GOD IN YOUR PERSONALITY

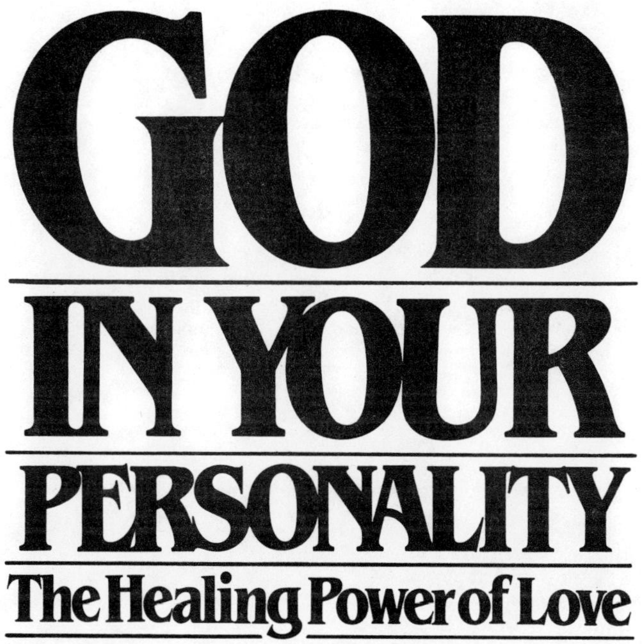

GOD IN YOUR PERSONALITY

The Healing Power of Love

Everett L. Shostrom
&
Dan Montgomery

ABINGDON PRESS
NASHVILLE

Library of Congress Cataloging-in-Publication Data

Shostrom, Everett L., 1921—
  God in your personality.
  Bibliography: p.
  Includes index.
  1. Christian life—1960–. 2. Christianity–Psychology. I. Montgomery, Dan 1946–
BV4501.2.S4518   1986   233.'5   85-23018

ISBN 0-687-14970-3 (soft: alk. paper)

MANUFACTURED BY THE PARTHENON PRESS AT
NASHVILLE, TENNESSEE, UNITED STATES OF AMERICA

Infinite Creator of us all,
Architect of planets and persons,
Author of the meaning of life . . .
We dedicate this book to you.

CONTENTS

1

ENCOUNTERING GOD

Our book has been born out of passionate concern to bring healing and wholeness to people. We want, as well, to build a theory of personality that is easy to understand, while at the same time being of great value in making sense out of life—and especially in illuminating that most mysterious and profound of all relationships, the encounter between you and God.

As Christians who are also professional psychologists, we believe that what we have to say has not come about by accident. Rather, it is the result of tough years of clinical training and work, combined with a deepening desire to be guided and led by the Holy Spirit—a merging of science and faith if you will.

But before we progress further, we want you to know us as persons and fellow seekers in the adventure of life. In order to do so, each of us has written a short vignette describing an experience in which our lives were touched by God. For each of us, the experience proved to be life-changing and has led to, among other things, the writing of this book.

In the Presence of My Enemies—Ev Shostrom

Destined originally to be an army of occupation, our 75th Division was instead committed to combat when the

Germans made their last attempt to reverse the tide of World War II. I was a brand-spanking-new 2nd lieutenant platoon leader. On December 13, 1944, my birthday, I went into combat with forty-eight men. When I was wounded seven weeks later, I had only eight men left.

Because of the desperately difficult conditions of combat in the middle of winter, that nearly two-month period was the most trying in my life. Again and again, my platoon was chosen to lead the wedge of the company into combat. Often we walked through six feet of snow. I was dead tired, and angry at the hunger, fatigue, and all the hardship of intense combat. Somewhere deep within I cried out to God to somehow touch me in this situation, but my prayers seemed only weak and scattered in the deafening din of artillery and machine-gun fire.

With hardly any hope at all, I motioned to my men to follow me into yet one more futile and devastating charge. Leaping out of my foxhole, I was halted in my tracks by a blast of enemy fire that sent me reeling. In those short seconds I thought myself dead. Only gradually did the blackness of unconsciousness give way to some awareness of what had happened.

I was all alone, among the dead bodies of many of my comrades. I couldn't move, but I did feel the steady trickle of warm blood over my cold and numb body. For a moment I thought I recognized a constellation, for the stars were beginning to come out. Then the sounds of approaching footsteps struck a new terror in my heart. "Where are you God!" I cried out within. The Germans now stood over me, several automatic rifles aimed at my head.

But they didn't fire, they only looked.

Within the hour, a larger perspective of the battle had emerged. My own troops had overrun the Germans at another point, and were now the victors. Soon German refugees started coming from the newly taken town and saw me, hurt and badly bleeding. I was so weak I couldn't even ask for assistance. Yet these men, who only hours ago I was trying to kill, voluntarily picked me up and carried me to a nearby German hospital. It had not yet even been taken over by U.S. military medical corpsmen. So, miraculously, I found myself being nursed back to health by Germans. My "enemies" cared for me even before my comrades could do so.

This was the most dramatic moment of my life. In a crazy war where values were turned upside down, I felt respected by a German nurse, who by his compassionate caring demonstrated to me the power and universality of God's love.

I have never doubted again the fact that God intervened in my circumstances to bring me health and life, and to reveal a new direction for my life.

I had accepted Jesus Christ as my Savior in my humble beginnings as a "soldier" in the Salvation Army. But even then something deep within, which I now recognize as the prompting of the Holy Spirit, was urging me toward a deeper comprehension of human nature and human relationships. Now I can see how God integrated those early promptings with the major happenings in my life, and I am still seeking to serve him in the ministries of counseling, teaching, and writing.

Before the war, I had been an accounting major at the University of Illinois. During my sixteen-month recuperation period in the military hospital, I sensed new inner guidance from the Holy Spirit that I was to enter the field of clinical psychology. Owing my very life to him, I gladly received the call.

As a professional psychologist for over thirty years now, I have counseled several thousand people, written eight books (some of the books have been translated into Arabic, Spanish, Swedish, and Chinese), developed six personality assessment instruments, and spoken in most states of the Union. My textbook, coauthored with Dr. Lawrence Brammer, is entitled *Therapeutic Psychology*. The text, used in over two hundred colleges and universities—including Yale and Harvard—is currently in its fifth edition. For the sixth edition, Dan Montgomery will join our writing team as coauthor. Already Dan and I have coauthored chapters in two recently released books: *The Holy Spirit in Counseling* (edited by Brock and Gilbert; Hendrickson Press, 1985); and *Handbook of Innovative Psychotherapies*, edited by Raymond Corsini (John Wiley, 1982).

As you can see, my life has been a very busy one, but I wouldn't have had it any other way, because it has been exciting and challenging as well. Also, I have had to lean on the Lord often, and to seek the inspiration of the Holy Spirit all along the way.

In this book Dan and I will share hundreds of secrets that our life journeys have yielded up to us. We call these secrets the facts of personality or the Laws of Living, because they are based upon *both* sound scientific research *and* trustworthy biblical principles. As you gain mastery of our theory and the special insights it gives to you, you will be able to make the change from mediocrity or stagnation into a genuinely Spirit-filled personality. This accomplishment is my warm wish for you.

The Rushing Wind—Dan Montgomery

I locked myself in a large room on the top floor of an old Methodist church. I didn't want to be disturbed on this warm, quiet, New Mexico summer night.

My heart was expectant. I was seeking God.

Ever since graduation from university that year, I had been filled with an urgency to reconnect with an old acquaintance—God. I had first accepted Christ in a personal way in a Baptist service at eight years of age. I had next rediscovered him in a Presbyterian retreat as a senior in high school. But the whole thing had kind of fizzled out by the time I graduated from college. In fact, try though I did, I never could seem to keep the awe and wonder of the conversion or rededication experience alive. I needed more power, more insight—more something.

So gradually I had drifted further and further, on over into agnosticism and even atheism for awhile. What my poor family had to put up with! If I wasn't an ardent Christian, then I was an ardent atheist. Oh well, it was just early training for my involvement in understanding the polarities which underlie all personalities. But I didn't know that back then, twenty years ago.

So as a college senior I daringly stated my view of life with the grand pronouncement that "God doesn't exist; we only project onto a Heavenly Father the care for us that we wish to believe in. The belief in God is an opiate to satisfy the universal obsessional neurosis for security and meaning"—this all, of course, a mixture of Freud and Marx and others.

But after graduation I underwent a compelling urge to find God again—if he was there. My life was empty. Being accepted as one of thirty-two students from fifteen hundred applicants to the University of New Mexico School of Medicine lost its luster. Graduating *summa cum laude* had no meaning. Life, in fact, was becoming awfully hard to live. I mean basic things like getting up in the morning.

Could it be that the Christ I had encountered at eight was indeed real—a risen Christ, an energetic presence within the personality that "makes all things new"? I had to find out.

For many months I was gripped with one essential concern: to rediscover God, or from a more personal point of view, to encounter him at a whole new level. Could the God of my youth handle the worldly-wise man I had become? Could he answer my tough questions? Was he even interested in a dialogue?

Day and night I struggled. I read the New Testament several times. I didn't like what I read—have faith, have faith, have faith! I didn't have any faith. That was my problem.

My first, deepest, and most sincere prayer that year was, "God, if you exist, do something! . . . and if you don't exist, then obviously this prayer is wasted and I'll do my best to cope."

From then till now, not only did he do "something," but he did and continues to do so many "somethings" that I don't think I'll ever get over it.

It was after the first few very special, very intimate "somethings" that God did in my life, that I locked myself in that upper room to get to a bottom line. I now knew to my satisfaction that he existed. I knew that he loved me. I knew that Christ knocks at the innermost door to the human heart, waiting expectantly for a response. And I had finally opened that door to him. But I longed for more—for the power, the compassion, the courage, the humility, the faith, and the vitality to do justice to his presence in me.

"O Lord," I prayed as I sat expectantly in the dark room, "I'm so thankful for how you've drawn me back to you. I want to walk close to you and serve you till my last dying breath. Please give me the power and the grace to do so."

Looking back on that quiet, reflective moment, I'm not sure what I expected God to do, but I certainly was not ready for what happened next. The roar of a mighty, rushing wind filled the room!

I would have been scared out of my wits except that such a soothing, sensitive love accompanied the noise that I felt bathed in love. The surge of warm, tingling feelings reached such a crescendo that I thought I'd explode. "Stop!" I yelled. And the sound and sensation immediately stopped.

I walked over to the windows, my old skepticism surging, to make sure that the wind I had just heard had not been from outside. It had not; the night was still. I became aware of the rapid throbbing of my own heart.

Now convinced that God in a very unusual way was touching me, I returned to the center of the room, sat down, relaxed, and began to pray again. "God, I'm sorry I got so scared. Go ahead. Let me feel your love . . . fill me with your power."

Exactly as before, the room filled with the surging sound of wind and my body was infused with a most profound sense of joy. How could such an ocean of power be so gentle, so caressing! Then, suddenly: fear. I couldn't stand for another moment the ecstasy of such a love. I shouted, "Stop!" And all fell silent.

After several minutes my breathing returned to normal. I spoke to the Lord: "I don't fully understand the meaning of this experience. I am amazed and awed. Your love and power go beyond anything I ever dreamed. I just want to build on this night, and learn to trust you throughout my life whether I have signs or not. Thank you for being so patient. I have a lot to learn. Good night."

With that I took a deep breath, found my way out of the darkened church, and drove home. "He loves me," I whispered to myself. "He is so near—and he loves me."

It's been almost two decades since that memorable night. And what I still tell people who have a hard time believing that God exists, or that Christ is risen, or that the Holy Spirit can fill the human personality, is: "Just pray this one simple prayer, 'God, I don't know if you exist or not, but in case you do, please do something special in my life so that I can know and believe.' "

But don't get the mistaken idea from all this that my walk with the Lord has been easy. Far from it. It has been at times turbulent, at times frustrating, at times inspiring, and at times precious beyond words. But I learned long ago that a decision to follow Christ is only the first step; walking the walk, and growing day by day, is the second.

It was years after he led me away from medical school that I was directed by the Holy Spirit to gain a master's degree in philosophy, and then a doctorate in psychology. After teaching psychology for five years in a Christian liberal arts college, I experienced a very perplexing and painful mid-life crisis—a major life transition that led to my current work in private practice, and in speaking and writing. In hindsight I can now recognize a wonderful thread of continuity that runs throughout my life. I praise God generously for his genius in guiding me to fulfill his will.

*   *   *   *   *   *   *

We decided to write this book as a shared statement of our Christian faith and as part of the mission we both feel to unearth the facts of human personality and to unravel the often tangled threads of interpersonal encounter. Our theory is simple in many ways, yet profound in others. For this reason we suggest you read it several times through, making abundant notes and markings for present and future reference. Our theory and its unique applications to your personality will greatly enhance your life.

EXERCISES

1. Reflect back on a time when you needed God. What were the circumstances? Are you continuing to build on the relationship with him that you began at that time? Relationships require continued desire, openness, and commitment. We suggest you spend a few concentrated moments today or tonight reestablishing your openness and desire for God.

2. If your connection to God is or has been diminished by doubt, worry, fear, unanswered prayer, guilt, procrastination, or anything else, then we suggest that you give God permission to love you anyway. Write down on paper all the reasons you don't feel close to him, and then tear the paper to shreds and throw it in the wastebasket. Now relax, for it is now God's move to reach you . . . watch what happens this week.

3. We stated at the beginning that our main purpose is to give you valuable insight into yourself and others. Write down in your diary or elsewhere the things that perplex, hurt, or befuddle you the most about yourself or people. Then look for ways that our theory clarifies the confusion and plots out new, direct ways for overcoming it.

4. Make it a point to mark this book with highlights and margin notes. (The greatest university in the world is your own private library.) Master the material. Muse over and digest it. Mark relevant sections for rereading months or even years from now.

2

YOUR GROWTH POTENTIAL

Life is richest when we realize that we are all snowflakes. Each of us is absolutely beautiful and unique. And we are here for a very short time.

—*Elisabeth Kübler-Ross*

All of us need God. And all of us are aware of our need at some time or another. As someone said, "There are no atheists in foxholes." But what if you do not wait for the inevitable crisis and open yourself to join forces with him now? To our way of thinking, "preventive Christianity" is more valuable than "crisis religion." But regardless of which way you choose to encounter God, the deeper question is, what will you do once you have met him? Will you grow? We hope so, and to encourage that growth, we will be presenting the *how*.

There is a particularly striking passage in Paul's letter to the Ephesians (3:16-19) which we will underscore to emphasize the growth-centered orientation that arises out of an encounter with God. Paul first speaks of the "glorious, *unlimited resources*" of God, and that from these resources "He will give you the mighty *inner strengthening of his Holy Spirit*" (v. 16 TLB, italics ours).

So, as pastors have often stressed, we are not spiritual orphans stranded without hope in a world devoid of meaning. The Holy Spirit *within* is God's personal agent for continuously prompting us toward creative coping with problems and steady growth toward the actualization of our individualized missions.

But there's more. "[I pray] that Christ may dwell in your hearts through faith; that you, being rooted and grounded in love, may have power to comprehend with all the saints what is the breadth and length and height and depth, and to know the love of Christ which surpasses knowledge, that you may be filled with all the fulness of God" (vv. 17-19 RSV).

Two things cited here are the warp and woof of a reliable psychology of personality and can provide you with a set of compass points for finding your way accurately in any relationship that you have. The first is that the Holy Spirit prompts you from within, from the core or innermost part of your being. And the second is that the power of Christ's love has a north, south, east, and west for potential development. He does not just send you off without a compass. That would be disastrous. When people have been fired by a Christian conversion, but remain infantile in understanding the true dynamics of personality and relationships, they often cause nothing but trouble. We hypothesize that even the devil would take little interest in such people, because they do enough damage on their own.

We have coined a phrase to describe the Christian who not only makes a decision to have Christ enter and vitalize his or her life, but who also continues to be open and desirous of inspired growth through life. The phrase is "the actualizing Christian." First we will expand the meaning of the word *actualizing* and then we will use the word and its many synonyms throughout the book.

The Synonym Finder, by J. I. Rodale, lists the following words to expand the meaning of *actualize:*

* make real   * embody
* personify   * make happen

* bring about   * work out
* compass   * carry out
* follow through   * consummate

Actualizing is a lifelong process, not a final state or a rigid ideal of perfectionism. It is a vision of how we can grow through the stages of life. Bernadette Vetter speaks of the journey of actualizing as "an opening of new doors, a becoming, a probing, a going inwards to my center, a developing of relationships . . . every arrival is a new beginning!" (*My Journey My Prayer*, p. 18).

The actualizing Christian grows by continually exploring, expanding, and revising his or her understanding of doctrine, Scripture, personal values, and openness to God throughout life. Faith requires an opening of ourselves to new ideas and experiences, and a willingness to let outgrown and partial ideas of truth die. The new wine of the Christian's Spirit-led life must continuously be put into the fresh wineskin of new attitudes, perceptions, and values. This is growth in the finest sense of the word. This is what Paul Tillich means by "the courage to doubt"—the courage to *entertain* differences or exceptions in the hope that we can learn new and more satisfying truth. Catholic philosopher Gabriel Marcel writes in *Creative Fidelity* (p. 190): "Authentic Christian thought is an open thought *par excellence.* . . . A real orthodoxy creates those conditions rooted in the supernatural which unfold the most spacious and unbounded horizons for human knowledge and action."

That's what we love about Christianity and one's personal walk with Christ—it is an adventure, not a tedious task.

Author's personal comment—Dan:
As I've said, before my conversion I didn't believe in God. Period. I thought life, death, disease, destiny—all

were random happenings in an impersonal universe. The year before encountering Christ I toured Mexico with some kind of hope of finding value or meaning to human life. But I was so objective about it that when one night I saw a man fall to the pavement with obvious respiratory problems, I didn't take the time to stop and give him artificial respiration. It didn't matter to me if he lived or died. I now hope that there was someone who cared enough to come to his aid.

But with Christ in my life I suddenly cared—a great deal—about everybody.

When I read a section in the book of James about laying hands on the sick and praying for their healing, I felt immediately ready to so so. And the first two people I happened to pray for were healed. One was a man in a small town in Texas, who had been laid off work for several years because of a lame hand. A surgeon at a renowned clinic, during a difficult operation, had accidentally cut this man's motor nerves. They told him he'd never use three of his fingers again. I preached in a Methodist church then in the man's hometown, and he called me afterward to his house.

"Do you really believe I can be healed?" he asked sincerely. "Yes," I replied with butterflies in my stomach. I took the hand and said the simplest prayer of my life: "Father, heal this hand in Jesus' name." Within seconds he opened the hand completely and kept staring at it as he flexed it open and closed again and again. I left him and his wife amidst tears and hugs.

The second dramatic healing occurred when I was staying overnight in a home in Lawrence, Kansas. At supper the mother had mentioned that her three-month-old son had heart problems and was scheduled for surgery in several weeks. I didn't pay much attention.

But later, around midnight, as I was absorbed in reading a book, a voice from deep within said, "Dan, go pray for the boy and he will be healed." In my usual fashion I ignored the voice. I never have liked being put on the spot.

In a few minutes the voice said the same words again. It got my attention. "Lord if that's you, I will stick my neck out and do what you say, but if it's not you we'll both look like fools." Silence. Then, a third and last time the message came.

Up I got, wakened the mom, got the boy, laid hands on, and prayed: "In the name of Jesus this boy is healed."

Having great respect for the medical profession, I added instructions to the mother. "Take this boy to the surgeon and do whatever that doctor says." She did. That week the surgeon examined the infant and called off the surgery. "The heart has healed itself," he told her. "There's no more hole."

Now the reason I'm telling you all of this is that I thought for awhile I was hotter than Oral Roberts. The thought definitely occurred to me to begin going up and down hospital wards healing people right and left, and thereby putting an end to the medical profession. Not so.

Growth required me to pray for numerous others over the years with just as much faith and fervor, but seldom with the same results. Some were healed slowly, for some the pain was taken away, and one actually died shortly after I prayed for her. These experiences provided growth—getting a larger and more flexible perspective, keeping faith, but also being humble and open to new and different outcomes.

The actualizing Christian learns throughout life by risking, experimenting, trying things out, and getting feedback so as to build an ever-enlarging sense of God's mysterious plans, purposes, and adventures.

In this open-ended and progrowth approach, there is a desire to always grow beyond one's prejudices and premature conclusions about life. In psychological terms, one develops an open perceptual field in which new configurations of meaning and interpretation constantly emerge. In religious terms, we learn to be sensitive to the heart and mind of Christ—and are easily prompted by the Holy Spirit.

Author's personal comment—Ev:

This past year several things happened to me so suddenly that I did not know which way to turn. I felt jarred and afraid. Facing a formidable series of lectures across the country, I learned that I was suffering from 50 percent blockage of the carotid artery from high cholesterol intake over the years, and that I might be facing imminent surgery if the problem couldn't be corrected through exercise and diet. I felt stunned to the core. Had God miraculously spared me from German machine guns only to give me over to arteriosclerosis later in life?

My wife, Dan and his wife, and I all spent time in prayer to try to discern God's will. I once again deeply yielded my life to Christ, so that I could learn what he was expecting of me and which direction I should go. Out of this surrender came a deep peace . . . a sense of the presence of the Comforter, the Holy Spirit. I reviewed the road I had traveled in life, and again asked God that if there was further work to be done, to heal me so that I could know the fullness of my journey completed.

Even though I feel worried occasionally, I have already begun to realize that God is answering our prayers, and that his hand is in all that is happening to me. A new nutritional program prescribed for me is building up my bodily resources, and a program of exercise coupled with relaxation is beginning slowly to counter the plaque in my circulatory system. I am thankful to God and to modern science because I believe that God works his wonders through the knowledge and insight that science reveals, as well as through his own direct intervention.

This experience has helped me understand again that God never promised us a rose garden, life without hardship and pain. I have grown deeper in faith ever since I faced the possibility of my own death. I have faith in Christ's acceptance of me despite my many sins. I am confident that my acceptance of Jesus as my personal Savior means that I will be with him in heaven whenever I may die. In the meantime, I intend to serve him all my days.

To conclude, the actualizing, growth-oriented Christian needs courage to embrace insecurity and doubt. As the apostle Paul says, we only see things now "through a glass, darkly" (1 Corinthians 13:12 *KJV*). Such a Christian is the opposite of the fanatic, who attacks with disproportionate violence those who disagree or suggest creative alternatives. The maturing Christian has the "courage to be" in spite of doubts, which are valued because they can help growth. We should not try to be like neurotic religious zealots, who try to build narrow castles of certitude defended with the utmost tenacity. Rather, we should continue to express and to ask, so that we can receive answers in our areas of doubt—knowing that some answers do not come easily. We should have faith that by asking, seeking, and knocking, we will eventually discover answers that make precious, personal sense in our lives.

As is suggested by Doctor Luke, recording Jesus' words, "keep on asking and you will keep on getting; keep on looking and you will keep on finding; knock and the door will be opened. Everyone who asks, receives; all who seek, find; and the door is opened to everyone who knocks" (Luke 11:9-10 *TLB*).

First of all there is commitment—to keep on with the

process. Second there is courage—to search for the open door. Third there is expectancy—that the door will be open. But through it all there is growth. There is adventure. There is the openness to be surprised by God. And there is the realization of all of our potential.

This unique potential is masterfully embedded in our genetic code, our early socialization, and the opportunities ever present during our lifetimes. This internal blueprint pushes, energizes, and guides us. But the journey toward fulfillment is never to be taken for granted. Thomas Merton, a Trappist monk, once said he felt he was "ascending the mountain of love on all fours and I don't know where . . . to look next." There will be real travail and a crucible of testing for anyone who desires to become a genuinely growing and self-actualizing Christian. But there will be real joy too—the joy of being what one is and becoming more of what one is called to be.

This kind of growth involves a full development of one's personality, along with a heightened responsivity to other people and to the spontaneous as well as long-term guidance of the Holy Spirit.

For this we turn to the "compass points of the self."

EXERCISES

1. In your own assessment are you a growing or stagnant Christian—or are you a combination of both?

2. How do you respond to the phrase, "the courage to doubt"? Does your religious orientation leave room to ask certain embarrassing questions, or to wrestle with certain doubts?

3. Are you personally more into self-expression or into adjusting your behavior to meet other people's expectations? Is there a possibility of any new

synthesis or balance between the two? Think in terms of specifics.

4. Do you believe in instantaneous sanctification and perfection, or do you see the need for growth over time in the context of your and other's imperfections? Why or why not?

5. Can you take the risk of authentic self-disclosure this week, telling another person of your less flattering qualities, as well as expressing your perceived strengths? Can you ask for and experience their understanding and prayer?

6. Contemplate the mighty words of Christ: " . . . keep on asking and you will keep on getting; keep on looking and you will keep on finding; knock and the door will be opened. Everyone who asks, receives; all who seek, find; and the door is opened to everyone who knocks" (Luke 10:9-11 *TLB*). How can you make your relationship with Christ and the Holy Spirit more dynamic and continuous?

3

COMPASS POINTS OF THE SELF

Man alone, of all the creatures of the earth, can change his own pattern. Man alone is the architect of his destiny. The greatest discovery of our generation is that human beings, by changing the inner attitudes of their minds, can change the outer aspects of their lives.

—William James

How many times have you been told that your Christian duty is to be holy and to grow in righteousness? We wish to translate these terms into clearer concepts. For now we can point out that *holy* means not only "separated unto God" but also "whole." And *righteousness* means not only "pure in one's dealing with others," but also relating "rightly" to them. The how of attaining wholeness of the personality and rightness in relating to others is our theme.

If you want to get somewhere that you have never been before, you need a map, along with specific instructions. Our map of the human personality is this: human beings can be described by four basic characteristics or polarities: love, assertiveness, weakness, and strength. A polarity always has a polar opposite and this design can be illustrated by a continuum that contains many connecting points between the two opposites. Day and night, dawn and dusk, and every second of every hour between midnight and noon, are examples of polarities. Noon is the opposite of midnight, but they are both intimately connected to each other in a larger, more whole context, called a day. Neither cancels out the other. Both are needed, and both have equal value and significance.

In the same way assertion (which implies standing against someone) is the opposite of love (which implies standing with someone), but both are required to make a healthy human relationship. Both ends of the continuum, as well as the many points in between, are required to give color, richness, and integrity to a human bond.

To love someone is to be close to him, often giving pleasurable "strokes," "warm fuzzies," or messages that he is regarded as being special. Love involves a warm, nonjudgmental empathy that reaches deep into the heart of the other. Parents often experience this feeling for their children; or spouses in vitalized marriages for each other.

We can expand this love polarity to say that people who are really maturing in Christlikeness experience a sort of tenderness for all of humanity—they can be touched emotionally by the melancholy of human suffering, and they try as best they can to remedy the situation whenever their personal choice can make a difference.

But closeness also means rubbing each other the wrong way from time to time. And then it becomes appropriate to move on the continuum from love to assertion and to say "ouch" or "that irritates me." This is the function that assertion serves in a relationship. If you do not tell someone how he or she is offending or hurting you, he or she remains in the dark about it, and your resentment builds over the weeks or years. We need to express our "little assertions" and keep them from building into more forceful feelings of indignation and anger. To express them takes courage. But it also means that we care enough to express our real feelings, and then to be open to the feelings of the other person. With new, current information, both partners can form a more updated, mutual, and trustworthy relationship.

One of the problems in many churches is the fear of open and emotionally honest communication. Many Christians are taught to suppress their real feelings, to keep smiling, and to remain polite and agreeable. These guidelines are all right as long as we do not really care about the quality of the relationship. But if we, like Jesus, do care about being transparent and open with those closest to us, then it becomes essential to communicate frequently and openly not only about our hopes, and joys, but also about our disappointments, needs, frustrations, and irritations. Only this emotional and spiritual honesty can form the right stuff for an enduring and endearing bond.

So assertion and love go hand in hand. And so does a second set of polarities, which we call strength and weakness.

For the Christian the word *strength* has multiple meanings. Reduced to its simplest level, it is the inner affirmation that our lives have great value. This is the Good News or gospel that Jesus came into the world to proclaim. It is why he did not humiliate the woman caught in adultery at her most vulnerable moment. He affirmed her instead, and it turned her life around.

Our lives are precious—irreplaceable. What Jesus is by nature, he enables us to become through grace and the new birth—sons and daughters of the living God. Theologian Adrian van Kaam writes: "We will see in eternal gratefulness how the inner spring of grace made our deepest self similar to Jesus. We will see how the spring inside us leaps up with dazzling splendor for all eternity" (*The Woman at the Well*, p. 57).

The maturing Christian has long ago settled the question of the true source of his or her identity, dignity, and strength—it is our spiritual bonding with the risen

Christ, made experientially real by the indwelling power of the Holy Spirit. As Paul said, "I can do all things through Christ which strengtheneth me" (Philippians 4:13 KJV). Or, perhaps even more understandable to the modern reader, the Modern Language Bible translates the same sentence as, "I have *strength* for every situation through Him who *empowers* me" (italics ours).

Strength is the dimension of personality that lets us take a stand for values or feelings we believe in. We do not have to think only in terms of dramatic acts of bravery, for more often there is a hidden side of strength that has to do with the way each of us lives in the most ordinary of circumstances. For instance, do we express our feelings, thoughts, and needs—even in the face of possible disagreement or rejection—in open and direct ways? Jesus did.

Strength enables us to recognize and face squarely the difficult, painful, or perplexing aspects of life. We can stand out in ways that represent our genuine, albeit sometimes misguided or faltering, attempts to approximate truth, justice, and healing love in the world.

But here is where strength intersects the last polarity in our theory: *weakness*. None of us represents truth infallibly. As John wrote, "If we say we have no sin, we deceive ourselves, and the truth is not in us" (1 John 1:8 RSV).

Peter was embarrassingly caught being stuck on the strength polarity, without a balancing acknowledgment of his human frailties and weaknesses, when he made his grand pronouncement at the Mount of Olives, "If everyone else deserts you, I won't. . . . I would die first!" (Matthew 26:33, 35 TLB).

An evolving maturity requires that each one of us, no matter how gifted, talented, or anointed, also accept that we are equally weak, often foolish, and make many mistakes.

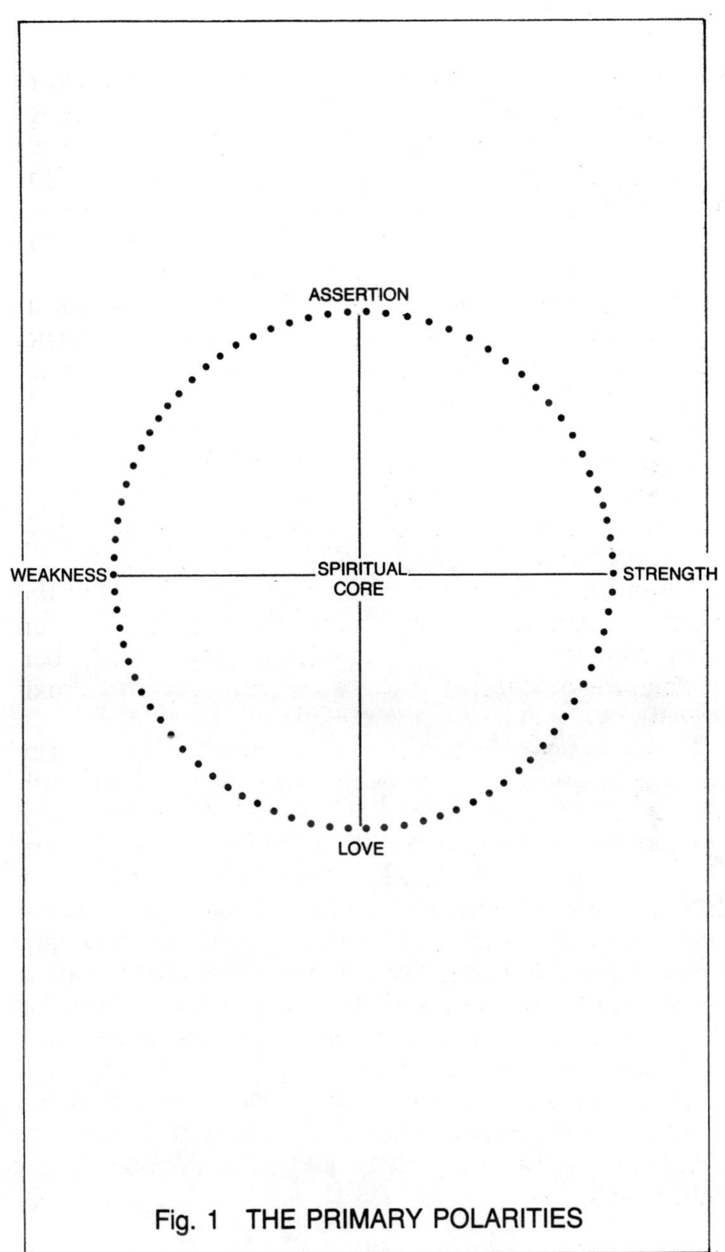

Fig. 1   THE PRIMARY POLARITIES

Artfully balancing our strengths and weaknesses, our virtues and shortcomings, and our talents and deficiencies enables us to thoroughly enjoy our strengths, while at the same time be humbly aware of, and therefore honest about, our weaknesses. This awareness, however, always draws us nearer to the Lord, who understands, accepts, and ultimately heals our weaknesses and transforms them through faith and growth into victory and wholeness. Isaiah (57:15 KJV) captures the dynamic rhythm in which weakness openly acknowledged can be turned by God into strength, revival, and renewal: "For thus saith the high and lofty One that inhabiteth eternity, whose name is Holy; I dwell in the high and holy place, with him also that is of a *contrite* and *humble* spirit, to *revive* the spirit of the humble, and to revive the heart of the contrite ones" (italics ours).

Through Weakness we approach God in need. Through Strength we approach him in praise. Through Assertion we approach him resolutely. And through Love we approach him heart to heart.

The best model for understanding the dynamic and rhythmic nature of personality (as shown in figure 1) is Jesus himself. Jesus embodied a quality of being that awed and moved people wherever he went. In his encounters with others he left healing, change, and renewal. He lived from his spiritual core and was able to express an intensity and authenticity of emotion appropriate to every situation. He could be *loving* enough to free and restore a woman caught in the act of adultery when her accusers wanted to stone her to death. He could be *assertive* enough to make a whip and physically drive the money changers from the temple. He could be *weak* enough to surrender to being put to death on a cross and buried in another man's tomb. He could be *strong* enough to live to the utmost his own values, and to rise from the grave a victor over death itself.

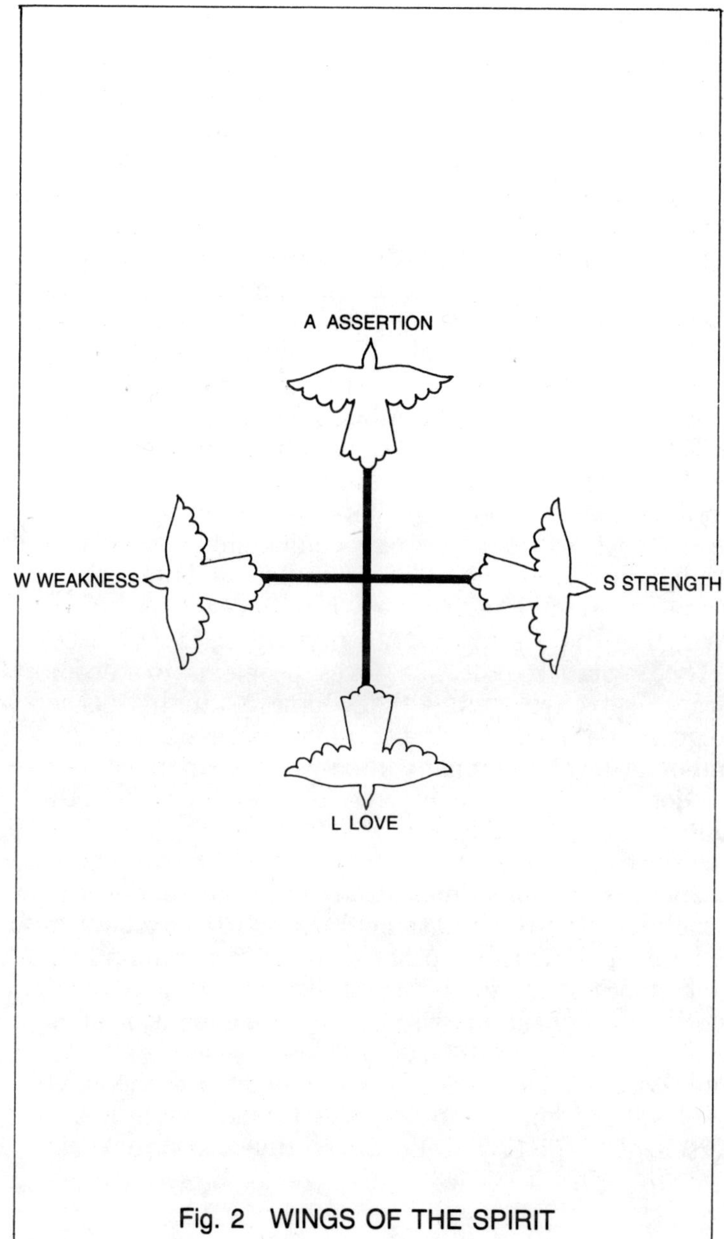

Fig. 2   WINGS OF THE SPIRIT

Jesus exhibited all the characteristics of a healthy and whole personality. He was not limited by partial perspectives, but had balance and grace and power—the same attributes that we need in our lives today. But how can we possibly emulate him? The answer lies in expanding the height, depth, and breadth of our personalities in the same directions he did. And what gives us courage and personal insight for doing this? The power of the Holy Spirit, the Comforter and Teacher who, Christ said, would indwell all who believed in him.

One of the New Testament symbols for the Holy Spirit is a dove (Matthew 3:16; Mark 1:10; Luke 3:22; John 1:32). For this reason we wish to expand the meaning of our theory of polarities by stating that it is the Holy Spirit working in and through us that vitalizes, energizes, and develops within us the primary compasslike expressions of a healthy personality. You can understand now, why it is that we sometimes refer to the primary polarities as "Wings of the Spirit," as shown in figure 2.

The invitation that God gives people is to become aware, sensitive beings like himself. Both sets of polarities—Love/Assertion, and Weakness/Strength—and every level of intensity in between them, need to be developed so that we can come to experience life in the fullest and most colorful way.

Instead of being one or the other, we need to learn balance: being sometimes strong and sometimes weak, sometimes assertive and sometimes caring. To follow the dynamism of the Holy Spirit's guidance and promptings, we cannot remain stagnant or rigid persons; hence, our continual emphasis on risk, growth, and expansion of the self.

Growth involves increased refinement of the skills involved in interweaving all the primary polarities of personality—the LAWS (Love, Assertiveness, Weakness, and Strength), if you will—onto the loom of your inner calling from God. A striking and irreplaceable work of art emerges over time—your unique identity, which is in essence the gift of God to you, and is to be used by giving yourself to God's universe.

Elizabeth, who first discovered psychology in one of Dan's classes and went on to codirect groups with Ev, and finally to gain a master's degree in marriage, family, and child counseling, tells the story of her journey of growth in a most interesting way. In her late thirties, having just added a third child to her family (and contemplating a fourth), she felt an inner urge to begin a college education. This brought into her awareness some painful issues in regard to self-identity, role confusion, initial conflict with her husband, and the frustration of finding and actualizing God's will. After a year of pursuing a new direction in her life, she wrote the following:

> Whoever was the first to make the analogy between caterpillars and butterflies and death and resurrection—old life and new life—must have had a "butterfly experience." And to a certain degree, so have I.
>
> Knots being untied; tight jar lids being loosened—it is freedom. It is freeing. It is the slow motion experience of leaping through a meadow with arms and legs in tune with the rhythm of life. But somehow the butterfly says it best, because of the cocoon experience.
>
> People seem to have more than one go-round with the cocoon. How did it start for me this time? Why did it start?
>
> I was happy as a caterpillar. Just a bit confined, that is all. I viewed myself, and others did, as fuzzy-wuzzy, problem free, happily married, financially secure, basking in the love of God . . . but I was not content.

I did not know myself. Actually, I did not even know that I did not know myself. And I certainly did not own my feelings. I had to move away from all those who unknowingly kept me as a pet caterpillar to learn the true situation. And that is why I ended up here at college.

Things have happened fast, which I like. But it has been a difficult, thrilling, laborious , joyous, arduous, and climactic year. There have been so many significant encounters. Every week of classes I have learned so much. But several things were of major importance.

Almost a passing comment by Dr. Montgomery turned a trickle into a flood last fall when he said, "Liz, I sense a lot of tension in you—and have since we first met." I could hardly believe it. Everybody knew how calm, cool, and collected I always was. I was not tense . . . how could he say that?

I was only going to school full-time, keeping my husband happy, preparing three meals a day, cleaning the house, taking my son to Cub Scouts and piano lessons, taking my daughter to Brownies and ice skating, and giving constant attention to my new baby girl! Tense . . . tense! How true! I had to face it. And so began a whole chain of discoveries.

I thought I was relaxed and learned myself I was tense. I thought I was well-adjusted and learned that I did not even know myself. I thought I was loving and learned that I was often indifferent. I thought I was social and learned that I was withdrawn. On the positive side, I thought I was dumb and learned I was intelligent.

At an earlier point in my Christian life, it would have seemed unspiritual to consider these things. But somewhere near the beginning of this year, I experienced a glorious assurance that God was in fact the One who had led me to this point—and he was leading me through!

For some reason, it seems that it is almost over. Or maybe it is the beginning of a new era building on what I have learned. I do know that I am more excited about life. I love my husband and children more than ever before. And I am more open to forming friendships with new people I meet. Most of all, I feel more comfortable being myself. In this year of growth I have come in touch with my own worth and potential.

Simply becoming aware was a great part of the answer. Perhaps that is because I wanted the change. I really do want to be a transparent person.

For now all I can say is that something deep is happening within me—and I love what is happening.

EXERCISES

1. Try a guided imagery exercise where you close your eyes and picture a compass with its points of north, south east, and west. Imagine for a moment the security the compass would provide you if you were lost in the woods and needed to find your bearings. Now substitute in your visualization the compass points of the self—Love, Assertion, Weakness, and Strength. Sense the new security that will be yours by utilizing these coordinates of personality during the next several weeks. Once mastered, they are yours for a lifetime.

2. Take the most perplexing and disturbing relationship you now have, and map out as clearly as possible how and where the other person (or you) is stuck on the

map of personality. Pray for guidance, and then try to think through new ways you can stretch yourself this month in personal growth to gain autonomy in this relationship. Concentrate especially on the particular chapter or chapters that bring clarity to the relationship, so that your anxiety and frustration can be changed to confidence and clear thinking.

3. Ask the Holy Spirit to reveal to you your most important or urgent need for personality growth. Speak to God about what you read all through the week. Listen for inner promptings and guidance. You are becoming a growing, more colorful, and wise person—deliberately. Be proud of yourself and also thank God for the opportunity.

4

WHAT BELONGS IN THE CORE?

You order all things graciously. You are the mystery unfolding cosmos and humanity. You are my homeland, my most original ground. Your Presence welds all things together. You are the caring love that carries me like mother earth does forest, flower, and tree. Your Presence alone is lasting home.

—Adrian van Kaam

Growth toward authentic personhood does not happen automatically. We cannot change ourselves suddenly and want to. Rather, real and enduring change is a gradual, steady process of becoming, like bulbs planted deep in a winter's garden that eventually bloom come springtime's warmth and light.

Inner growth is nurtured by the courageous acceptance of our whole being—strengths and weaknesses, irritations and moments of tender caring. If we take growth for granted, however, it may never occur at all. The context for our spiritual and personality growth is a trusting openness to God as a real and active Heavenly Father in our lives.

Author's personal comment—Dan:
One day when I decided it was time to take the training wheels off my five-year-old daughter's bicycle, I was struck by something she said. She felt definitely afraid of trying herself out, and the fear was warranted because she would have taken some brutal falls without my

39

assistance. So we had to figure out a way for her to utilize my support while at the same time stretching her abilities into new areas of mastery.

"Hold my hand, and I'll run alongside of you while you pedal," I said. She thought for a moment and then replied, "No, Daddy, I want you to hold my neck and push from behind . . . if I hold your hand I could let go, but if you're holding me I know you'll never let go."

Over the next three weeks of practice I was a bridge of trust back to her inner core. I held her while she experimented with all the complicated subleties of balance and equilibrium. But a day came when she suddenly eased out ahead of my hold and my push. Like a jet pilot breaking the sound barrier, she smoothly and confidently took over the controls.

I thought to myself, "Wow . . . there she goes!" And then I thought, "What if she hits a bump or a rut!"

I don't know if God feels excited when he trusts us with free will and individual choice. But I do know that if he didn't let us try out our wings now and then, we'd never mature at all.

Growth happens only with practice, concentration, and determination. Perhaps the courage to grow is one of the greatest of Christian virtues. Growth means heightening your awareness of the challenges and meanings that life is calling you to embrace. It means moving beyond present limitations toward actualizing future possibilities. It means gaining access to the inner, spiritual resources of the core of your being.

The spiritual core is an individual's God-given personhood, God's presence within. As Jesus said, "Behold, the kingdom of God is within you" (Luke 17:21 KJV). The Holy Spirit dwells here. The core reflects the fact that you are made in the image of God, and share with God the capacity for awareness, self-identity, choice, responsibility, and intimacy. Whether that potential is fully realized during the course of your life depends on how faithful you learn to be in following the wisdom of the core.

Author's personal comment—Ev:

For thirty years of my professional theorizing as a psychologist, I puzzled over this question of the core, the innermost source of identity and inspiration. During those years I put together a complex theory of personality that explained just about everything but the core.

I knew all about the polarities of the personality—the compass points of the self. I knew all about the ways in which people manipulate each other in self-defeating ways, and how neuroses and personality disorders rob people of their true potential. In fact, I wrote a book on this subject called Man, the Manipulator, *which sold over a million copies.*

Year after year I had master's and doctoral students do theses and dissertations advancing scientific knowledge deeper and deeper into the structure and dynamics of personality. And what I learned did prove to be of great value to several thousand patients I counseled. But still the question haunted me—"What goes in the core of personality?"

When I first met Dan about ten years ago, I felt a little uncomfortable with his outspokenness about God and the Holy Spirit. In the years of my youth in Illinois, it was considered rather rude to speak openly about one's religious beliefs or experiences. But Dan seemed adamant that psychology's deepest connection with religion was through the Holy Spirit—an active, vitalizing Presence in a believer's life.

After some months of soul-searching on the subject, it suddenly occurred to me quite forcefully: "The Holy Spirit belongs in the core!" I say belongs, because as a therapist I am quite well experienced in how other human energies can dominate the core of the self—useless worrying, fear or anxiety, guilt or shame, laziness or lack of motivation, apathy or indifference, depression, or hostility and alienation.

But these energies are uninvited guests, or better yet, invading aliens who break into the core like robbers in the night. They need to be ousted, and thank God, modern psychotherapy has a wide range of effective tools for accomplishing this. But what happens after these enemies of the human spirit are ousted? What is there to fill the vacuum? The Holy Spirit.

Ever since I was struck by this insight I have trusted God to be an invisible, but active agent in finding his way back into an alienated core so that he can work with great but gentle force from within.

Aristotle expressed a basic aspect of actualizing in his concept, *entelechy*. A root derivative of the word is *tele*, from *telos*, which refers to a thing's end or purpose. This insightful Greek philosopher viewed everything in the world as moving dynamically in the direction of completion, fulfillment, and actualization. Throughout the process, he believed that there existed a vital link between a person's or thing's actual characteristics at a given moment, and what would ultimately characterize and uniquely define it as a fully developed entity.

For instance, the acorn has within it the potential of becoming an oak tree. But it is only through the process of growth over time that the tiny acorn is able to carry out its mission to express its essence fully as a mature oak.

The powerful idea behind entelechy that has so much meaning to us as Christians is that the ultimate end or purpose toward which the acorn is developing is embedded in the acorn itself. The internal blueprint pushes, energizes, and guides the acorn all along the way. In much the same way the person who is rooted in God is being transformed over time into the unique individual that he or she was created and called to be.

Paul Tillich, a Christian theologian who fled Nazi Germany under Hitler's reign, defined religion as "man's ultimate concern." It is what has deepest and most pervasive influence in one's life. He also referred to the Holy Spirit as the "depth dimension of personality."

Perhaps this discussion will cast in a new light the passionate plea of the Psalmist to "*taste* and *see* that the Lord is good" (Psalm 34:8 RSV, italics ours). Becoming an aware and growing Christian involves learning to discover, affirm, and trust God's presence within us. As Bonhoeffer has expressed in *Ethics,* it is a coming home to one's Origin. It is slipping into the tailor-made clothing of one's original spiritual calling. In our words, it is accepting God's gracious invitation to become whole and rightly related to others and to God.

As we have already pointed out, this process is often slow and gradual, for fear, defensiveness, apathy, pride, or anger are tenacious tenants who are most reluctant to abandon the personality. But given time, even in harsh conditions, the God-inspired and Spirit-filled personality will still bring forth its bloom in due season. This is a tribute both to the resourcefulness of God and the openness of the person.

Many people have lost contact with God and with the spiritual core of their being. They no longer trust the inspired impulses from within. Instead, they take orders from their surroundings—from the media, from authority figures, from peers, from economic pressures, from fads, from gurus, or from an egocentric rather than core-centered self. There are instances, of course, when tradition, authority, society, or an enlightened teacher can assist an individual in beneficial ways. However, following the mentality of the crowd and the ways of the world often leads to spiritual death and stagnation of the personality.

In coming home to the core, to the presence of God within us, we gradually learn to give up our defensive style of living, which has been based on arrogance, anxiety, alienation, or apathy. We adopt instead a growth-oriented life-style based on openness, a desire to find God's path, and determination to be true to our inner beings. This determination implies firmness, but also flexibility.

We wish at this point to make clear that what we as psychologists refer to as the *core*, Scripture refers to as the heart. The word *heart* is used in Scripture as the seat of life or strength; hence, it means mind, soul, spirit, or one's entire emotional nature and understanding. It is also used to refer to the center or inner part of a thing.

The core, or heart, means the depth dimensions of personality. Important aspects of the core self include:

* trust in your Inner Supreme Court—the conscience that the Holy Spirit creates—for decision-making and life-style.

* the ability to use your intelligence in an open-minded and unprejudiced way.

* the willingness to feel and communicate a full range of emotions including love and assertion, and weakness and strength.

* respect for being a worthwhile and original person.

* trust in your inner promptings, hunches, and intuitions—for the growing person these often correspond with God's will.

* an openness in daily life to the mysterious ways that God may be working in your life.

* the courage to be a person-in-process, a work of art always in the making by the grace of God.

* determination to learn to accept, understand, and channel basic human energies such as sex and aggression into constructive outlets.

* sensitivity toward and value of all human life, as Christ modeled.

* an inner attitude of prayer without ceasing, in the sense of deeply desiring God's will to be done in your life, and his Presence to comfort and assist you.

In an age of technology such as ours, it may be difficult to accept that some things, such as wisdom, the capacity to love, the courage to be oneself, and the sensitivity to actualize one's spiritual destiny—cannot be reduced to a prefabricated, "instant" package.

One of the paradoxical aspects of personal growth is that it can never be forced. An invitation can be given. Consequences of choice can be made clear. But only inner self-determination can make the decision. Furthermore, every person must grow at his or her own pace. It is important to realize that you cannot force your growth! Rather, you have to combine commitment, courage, patience, and prayerful openness to the growth process. Some things you may never overcome. Others you outgrow so fast that it surprises you. Still others will have to be worked on for a lifetime to get the results you long for.

The key is a *vision* of the need to grow, to transcend your present limitations and liabilities. The next step is to get in touch, and stay in touch, with your core self, asking God to help you every step of the way. By living more and more of your life from the core, as opposed to silly or superficial or pretentious living, you will be encountering the Lord day and night, both consciously and unconsciously, with the deepest promptings you can recognize and feel that are your "heart's desires."

Listen to this passionate and perceptive passage from the Psalmist: "Trust in the Lord, and do good . . . . Take delight in the Lord, and he will give you the desires of your heart. Commit your way to the Lord; trust in him, and he will act" (Psalm 37:3-5 RSV).

The Holy Spirit works best and most easily within the person who is growing and flowing from the core, because that person is open to being prompted, educated, corrected, inspired, challenged, comforted, loved, directed, and finally fulfilled by God.

To trust God is to be enabled to trust yourself at the very core of your being.

What gives us all hope, once we understand it, is that none of us lives from the core all the time, or perhaps even most of the time. Even so, once we have been grasped by God's affirmation of us, we experience love at the very heart of all things—a love that cannot be denied and will never let go of us. And the power of that love begins to make all things in this partial and fragmented world whole again.

Paul expressed the profundity of this life-giving, life-affirming love as follows: "For I am convinced that *nothing can ever separate us from his love*. Death can't, and life can't. The angels won't, and all the powers of hell itself cannot keep God's love away. Our fears for today, our worries about tomorrow, or where we are—high above the sky, or in the deepest ocean—*nothing will ever be able to separate us from the love of God* demonstrated by our Lord Jesus Christ when he died for us" (Romans 8:38-39 TLB, italics ours).

EXERCISES

1. Get yourself into a private, safe place, without a clock, and without any other disturbing elements. Stretch

out fully on a comfortable chair or sofa. Take in an especially deep breath, and then let all tension melt and flow out of your body and mind. Now search your mind for some object with which you have personal experience, something that requires gradual growth and regular nurture to reach maturity. It could be your kitten, a plant, the front lawn, the making of a home out of a house, the raising of a child, the shaping of an oil painting, the enjoyment of a hobby, the deepening of a friendship, the toning of your body, the starting of a business, the creation of a casserole, the writing of a book, or the nurture of a family. Whatever the object you choose, let your imagination dwell on the process that brings this object from inception to completion. Repeat again and again in your mind the idea, feeling, and sensation of process . . . process . . . process. Let the feeling sink deeply into your awareness. Experience firsthand through this exercise how a process encompasses the essential steps of getting from a beginning to an end. Notice the feeling of pacing in the process—the sense that the time frame for many things cannot be hurried too much or delayed too long without causing harm. Now picture yourself as a person in the process of personality growth. See yourself as relaxed, committed to constructive change, and gaining new mastery every week and year.

5

PARTIAL PERSONALITIES

The mystics, in claiming that God is to be discovered in the self, are well aware of what they are saying. It is by neglecting the self that so many people have become really incapable of finding God.

—Ignace Lepp

If you came to us for personal sessions to get a better overview of your personality and life situation, we would first do three things: interact with you for an hour or so, give you one or two personality assessments, and have you fill out a multi-dimensional life history questionnaire.

We would try to know you as fully as possible, and expect you to be self-disclosing and honest in return. Without openness and honesty there can be no catharsis or healing. But we would not leave you stranded there, feeling alone and vulnerable. During further sessions we would stand with and for you, merging our resources and energies with yours to find out what is blocking your growth, in order to remove the obstacle, and set you on your way again.

Good therapy teaches a person to become more and more self-reliant and self-trusting. And that is what we believe God wants to happen through our profession.

Recently in group therapy with Ev and Dan, a forty-year-old woman declared her frustration with life. Sarah said, "Next week I am going to a twenty-year reunion of my high school class. Only I am terribly

48

embarrassed because I have accomplished exactly nothing in the last twenty years!" Though she had raised several children, she still felt lacking because in many ways her life had been completely dominated by her possessive and dictatorial husband.

She had tried many tactics over the years, including fighting, pouting, serving, or keeping sullenly silent. Now all feeling for her husband Jeff was gone, and while the couple continued to occupy the same house, they were indeed emotionally divorced.

An important reality the group fed back to Sarah was the possibility that the next twenty years did not have to be a grim repeat of the first twenty. People urged her to find her strength within to change things. But she would have to give up her partial perspective of helplessness and passivity. This was hard for her to believe—helplessness was the way she had been trained from childhood to respond to life. Her daddy was a Marine. He loved all the kids, but the only way he knew to relate to them was by giving orders and handing out cruel consequences if his orders were not followed. Her father was also a devoted Christian, but he was stuck on what we shall soon classify as the *Critical Perspective.*

And as for his daughter? No matter what she did it was never good enough. For Sarah, his love never came through. Only the message that her wants, feelings, dreams, and ideas did not matter came through. She became stuck in the *Helpless Perspective.*

What did Sarah's mother do through all this? She lived a thousand heartaches because she herself felt helpless to intervene. She did her best to please and placate the tyrranical dad, but nothing worked, and he always yelled at her as well. She was living out the *Compliant Perspective.*

The chaplain of her father's marine base had been consulted on several occasions by the family. He lacked the training necessary to bring therapeutic intervention to such a dysfunctional family, and only succeeded in making both Sarah and her mother feel guilty for not submitting to the authority of the "man of the house." The chaplain, who was living out the role of the *Striving Perspective*, always had quick and easy answers for how others ought to behave; but his suggestions did not arise from empathy and insight. His advice came from a need to dictate how others should think and be.

The root of the problem in all interpersonal relation-ships—whether we are speaking of communication between spouses, parents and children, supervisors and subordinates, clergy and congregation, or Sarah's fam-ily—is the *partial perspective* of the personalities involved.

Sarah took the encouragement of fellow soul-mates in group therapy to heart. She learned quickly how dynamics in her family as she grew up had cast her in a victim mold. With new inner strength she asked both her parents to enter family sessions with us.

It took several months, but Sarah's dad finally realized that he had been for years an authoritarian personality who knew only how to take and give orders. He learned that how he handled marines on the base ought to be quite different from the way to nurture, inspire, and raise a family in his home.

Sarah's mom made a firm decision to develop herself, instead of believing what her husband had for years told her—that she was "a nothing, a stupid woman, a dimwit, and an idiot." She began to handle affairs with the outside world—fixing the washer, having the fleas exterminated, changing a room into a den, and even buying a new car—competently.

Sarah's dad grew more tender—gradually! And her mom gained more strength—slowly! Both mom and dad stretched themselves from the polarity and partial perspective they were stuck on to the opposite polarity—thus creating greater balance within their own personalities and in their relationship to one another.

Though at first very threatened by his wife's new assertiveness, Sarah's dad later came to treasure it because it took many burdens off his shoulders, and gave him the calm assurance that another competent person was helping to run their household. Likewise he learned to accept Sarah's blossoming selfhood, without trying to undercut her as he had done for most of her life.

Being a witness to so much genuine change finally caused Sarah's husband, Jeff, to let go of his arrogant dictatorship over her. The emotional divorce gave way to a new and fresher discovery of one another that is growing deeper as of this writing. At the last therapy session Sarah's own family and her family by marriage stood together and wept happy tears. We took turns saying spontaneous prayers.

Moving from partial perspectives to whole and wholesome personalities is not an easy aim or accomplishment. It is often difficult, tedious, frustrating, seemingly impossible, and yet, suddenly it is unexpectedly there. This comes from the grace of the Holy Spirit being with and for us in our times of deepest need. We will say much more about that grace in closing chapters.

Sarah let us read the journal of written prayers she logged during the one and a half years of therapy. We found them to be especially thought-provoking, and wish to include them here as a tribute to Sarah:

* Lord, take hold of my heartaches and turn them into an opportunity for growth. Give me courage to change.

* God, help me learn to assume responsibility for myself, because I have an awfully hard time doing so.

* Enable me to develop an inner independence, without rebelling against someone or something—a sense of inner-direction when I am most quiet with you.

* Cleanse me of my negative thinking. These defeating thoughts stick to me, like leeches clinging to a person walking through swamp water, and they need to be pulled off. Let me grow beyond my rigidities—those prison bars that make me feel safe but keep me from living.

* Inspire me to cast off my fear of feeling, and to acquire a spontaneity of feeling, an awareness and aliveness of feeling, whether in respect to love or assertion, joy or sadness, self-respect or vulnerability.

* Create in and through me wholeheartedness: to be without pretense, to be emotionally sincere, to be able to put my whole self, most of the time, into my work, my relations to Jeff and the children, my feelings, and into my openness to you.

* Let me exercise my human freedom to actualize the very best of my talents, gifts, and uniqueness.

* Teach me to confess to you my faults, blunders, avoidances, and excesses, to accept your forgiveness and forgive myself. Help me never to feel that I have gone too far to know your forgiveness and faith in me.

* Well up within me a praise and thankfulness that does tribute to all that you are and all that you are always doing within my personality.

* Help me to forgive others with honest compassion, and to want their highest good even if they have hurt, wronged, or offended me.

Sarah's prayers, therapy, and stick-to-it-iveness turned a defeating disaster into a maximum miracle.

Now let us look at partial perspectives and personality disorders that can overtake the rest of us if we are not actively, consciously seeking God's inner growth in our lives.

In the next several chapters we will discuss in substantial depth the major ways that people, Christian and non-Christian alike, get stranded and stuck with partial personalities that make further growth impossible or at least highly improbable. You will quickly see and understand how this ties in with our theory of personality, for every person is moving one way or the other, upward toward Spirit-led actualization, or downward toward stagnation and Spirit-defying alienation.

Author's personal comment—Ev:
I realize that our concept of the Holy Spirit as energy in your life may not have much meaning for some readers. But I invite you to consider with us the possibility that the Holy Spirit—this mysterious energy that may be difficult to understand—is the personal Presence and source of inspiration for growth and fulfillment within human beings.

Even some of our Christian readers may have difficulty accepting this premise, because the Holy Spirit has sometimes been viewed as the vague third member of the Trinity who is spoken of in the Apostles' Creed but not experienced directly in daily life.

Looking back now over a good forty years, I see rather clearly how the Holy Spirit gathered me out of that deadly war scene in order to set my feet on the solid ground of what has become my life's mission: to illuminate as best I can the dynamics of personality and interpersonal relations. And my relating to God, whether through tender openness or human stubbornness, whether through proudest strength or most painful weakness, has become part and parcel of my theory of what it means to be human in an open and actualizing way.

It is my present firm belief, as I approach sixty-three years of age, that the Holy Spirit can give us the comfort and the power to live life openly, not from a fearful hiding place. "For God hath not given us the spirit of fear; but of power, and of love, and of a sound mind" (2 Timothy 1:7 KJV).

If you are seriously or even moderately underdeveloped as a person, then you are in for trouble no matter with whom you live or work. You have holes in your personality—blind spots that set you up for distorted self-expression and garbled conclusions about what others are trying to communicate to you. Many of life's miseries are optional, but only for those who choose growth and insight rather than using the same old partial perspective year after year. And the fastest way we know to achieve genuine growth and change, to move toward wholeness, is to master our theory of personality and put it to immediate use in your life.

The next four chapters are the substance of our theory. Take your time in thinking through the compass points of your own personality, then piece together this new knowledge to gain an overview of the personality profiles of those around you. With new knowledge comes freedom—freedom to journey intelligently toward greater wholeness, and freedom to evolve your relationships with others with more forethought and wisdom.

EXERCISES

1. Do you have at least one to three friends to whom you can bare your soul and lay things on the line? If not, then why not try during the next one to three months

to invite someone of your choice into a deeper relationship? It is not easy to become a soulmate. But if we never take risks, we end up alone and undeveloped. Realize and accept ahead of time that at some point you will most likely be hurt, disappointed, or misunderstood—an occurrence common both to Christ and to all humanity. Accept it at the beginning so that it will not and cannot deter you. Reach out anyway. Interpersonal skill is as much an art as it is a science. Actively apply the personality principles you are mastering as you read and study. And practice, practice, practice! The rewards of learning to connect emotionally, intellectually, and spiritually to another person are tremendous, as well as being a good part of what life is all about.

2. Ask several people this week to describe how they honestly experience you. What do they perceive as your strong and weak points? Learn to accept flattering and critical feedback alike, as you seek greater wholeness. Ask God's guidance in bringing into your life people who likewise value maturity and authenticity. Become willing also to stimulate the growth of others by utilizing your own growing skills from the Love/Assertion polarity. Enjoy your new freedoms and challenges.

3. Become a student of life. Start going beyond the superficial level of conversation into deeper and more probing areas. Disclose more of your private, emotionally colored self, and balance this by asking others to do the same. By relating deeply with people, you will learn to understand and think clearly about identity crisis, defense mechanisms, differences between the core and the superficial self, and developmental stages in

life. Brainstorm with them to discover how both of you can grow in areas of need. Strike a balance between talking and listening. Work for mutually fulfilling relationships. Learn to observe the interactions of other people in restaurants, at airports, at times of emergency, playing sports, or in any other type of encounter. Most of all learn from everything that happens to you. Turn it all into depth experience, astute insight, and mature overview.

4. Read the many books, which can be located in the bibliography, that we mention. This is the background homework you can do privately, and that nobody necessarily knows about—except God. Trust the Holy Spirit to call your attention to certain books that are keys to your growth all along life's journey. If you are a slow reader, do not be discouraged. Be creative. Utilize cassettes or videotapes, take a speed reading course, or just practice reading regularly until you become good at it! Whatever you read or do, learn, learn, learn!

6

THE COMPLIANT PERSPECTIVE
(LOVE POLARITY)

No matter how much we love a person, accept him, give him support, have warmth and affection for him, no matter how much we help him in so many ways, unless we can actually call him forth so that he is himself exercising the uniqueness God gave him, then the love is incomplete; he is less than fully human.

—Gordon Cosby

To heal the suffering soul and to generate a powerful picture of what it means to be both stranded in a partial perspective or freed up to become whole, we have organized a massive amount of research, clinical experience, and Christian teachings into four simple and easy to master discussions. Each discussion deals with one of the four compass points of the self that together form the LAWS (*Love, Assertion, Weakness, Strength*) of personality.

You will find yourself and everyone that you know described in these LAWS. You will see how you may have come to be stuck in a partial perspective by overusing just one, instead of all four, dynamic polarities of personality. You will also be shown how to get unstuck, and how to become a whole person. Because of our unique organization, these facts of personality can be remembered by both your conscious and unconscious self throughout life. You will always be able to size up situations and people according to these LAWS. Far from being blind to the forces that shape or influence your or anyone else's personality, you will become extremely aware, and other people may even come to you for that knowledge. Most of all, your own life will improve in every way, and you will, on purpose, alleviate most of life's miseries and maximize much of life's adventure. As you grow consciously you will become a Spirit-filled personality.

If you function mainly out of a partial perspective, you cannot help but experience a great deal of confusion and frustration in your relationships with others. One of our favorite sayings is that "most of life's miseries are optional." It will not take you long to see what we mean.

Healthy interpersonal relations can only arise from healthy intrapsychic wholeness. Disturbed relationships are related to "blind spots" in self-awareness. Knowing yourself and knowing you have the God-given ability to be whole, gives you the right to relate better with God and others.

Many psychologists would agree with a definition of personal growth as "making the unconscious conscious." We agree, but for Christians it might better be understood as "allowing the Holy Spirit to influence behavior from deep within." The point with which everyone agrees is that growth makes the partial more whole.

Author's personal comment—Ev:
One of my observations over the past thirty years of clinical work is that the Holy Spirit becomes an active force in the lives of people who are seeking truth and searching their souls. If you want more out of life, God is immediately there to facilitate your search. Sometimes he is there in obvious, miraculous ways—and sometimes he is there in sensitive, subtle ways. But he is always there. Even in the darkest, most terrifying moments when we

feel that there is no hope, no meaning, nothing special for our lives anymore.

Above all in my therapeutic work, I seek to create a new openness in my clients. An openness to life. An openness to listen more accurately to the messages from within. An openness to learn from everything that happens.

I find myself in deep agreement with Carl Jung (Carl Jung Speaking, 1977, pp. 74-75, emphasis ours): "Try to understand the will of God: the remarkably potent force of the psyche. It is all there. The kingdom of heaven is within you. *This is a great psychological truth. Christianity is a beautiful system of psychotherapy. It heals the suffering soul . . . It is not of vast importance that I make a career or achieve great things for myself. What is important and meaningful to my life is that I shall live as fully as possible to fulfill the divine will within me."*

In presenting the four primary ways that Christians, or anybody else, get stuck, we wish to use the categories of the Compliant Perspective (Love polarity), the Critical Perspective (Assertion polarity), the Helpless Perspective (Weakness polarity), and the Striving Perspective (Strength polarity).

To ground our theory of personality in state of the art diagnostic literature (which will be extemely useful to professional religious clergy, and to lay readers strongly involved with helping people), we will show how each of our four partial personalities can be correlated to a major personality disorder found in the *Diagnostic and Statistical Manual of Mental Disorders,* (3rd ed.), 1981 (referred to hereafter as *DSM III*). This is why we refer to the "facts of personality" — not conjectures, impressions, or educated guesses—but *facts* as trustworthy as the fact that stepping in front of a speeding truck will get you maimed or killed. Figure 3 illustrates the correlation.

Sometimes there is fear of seeing certain kinds of facts

POLARITIES	PARTIAL PERSPECTIVES	DSM III CATEGORIES	"STUCKNESS"	ACTUALIZING GROWTH
$\underline{L}$ LOVE	Compliant	1. Histrionic 2. Dependent	Pleasing and Placating	COMPASSION
$\underline{A}$ ASSERTION	Critical	1. Paranoid 2. Antisocial	Intimidating and Blaming	CONFRONTATION
$\underline{W}$ WEAKNESS	Helpless	1. Avoidant 2. Schizoid	Withdrawing and Numbing	EMPATHY
$\underline{S}$ STRENGTH	Striving	1. Compulsive 2. Narcissistic	Competing and Controlling	ESTEEM

Fig. 3 OVERVIEW OF "STUCKNESS" VS. GROWTH

about ourselves, but our position is that the facts are friendly. You can only be blessed, never harmed, by these facts. Our suggestion is that a certain degree of anxiety is OK if one is to grow. Let's call it normal anxiety. It is like coming out of a dark cave and temporarily feeling disoriented before our eyes adjust to the light from the sun. But, once adjusted, we are thrilled by a majestic world where we no longer prefer darkness—we have outgrown it and it serves no further useful purpose. Instead, we want to see things as they really are, and we can even feel proud of the fact that courage rather than fearful hiding describes our life. After awhile we become accustomed to seeing with enlightenment, and our temporary and fleeting fear is permanently replaced by the joy of seeing!

The first partial perspective that we want to look at is the Compliant Perspective. It results from getting stuck on the Love polarity. In the *DSM III* it is referred to as a combination of the Histrionic and Dependent personalities (see figure 3).

As Christians we constantly hear how important it is to love other people. We hear how Christ loved us so much that he gave his life to set us free from sin and judgment. We hear how the Holy Spirit will fill our hearts with love so that anyone who knows us will be touched and inspired by our love—the one most distinct quality that is said to make a Christian different from other people.

All of this is true enough. However, if taken as the whole truth for how personality is to be expressed, it fails the test. To show nothing but love becomes the neurotic rigidity of pleasing and placating others so that they will never disapprove of us. And with this sole principle dominating the personality, we cannot help but be sucked into a neurotic web of depending too much on other people's approval of us, and not enough on our own inner direction, as revealed by the Holy Spirit.

Jesus often took stands against the whims of crowds and individuals who were trying to pressure him into being something that he was not. At times he asserted himself in direct opposition to the desires and expectations of others. He was following a more inward voice. We need to model his courage.

It's not that loving is wrong; it's just that unbalanced loving is weak and ineffective. Loving without assertion is self-defeating. If you can only say yes to people's needs and expectations, and can never say no without feeling guilty, then you are unbalanced.

The harmonious functioning of an individual with others and with society depends upon the command: "Thou shalt love thy neighbour as thyself " (Matthew 19:19 *KJV*). Not more, but also not less. And notice that it says to love your neighbor *as well as* you love yourself—not *instead of* loving yourself! It's both/and, not either/or!

Here is Mary Sue's interpretation of what we have just said (see figure 4). She lived well into her forties out of the Compliant Perspective. Then she finally learned to understand her life from a new point of reference: the four polarities. Everything changed—slowly but with real joy and relief. Here is a bit of her story in her own words, and it shows how our psychological experiences in childhood can influence negatively or positively our spiritual understandings in adulthood.

I remember as a little girl of six my dad telling me he wished I'd been a boy. I felt awful. I felt guilty for disappointing him. I gladly would have changed myself had it been possible, so that he could love me.

Strange how those early experiences with my daddy left me with such deep feelings of being "*not OK.*" I realize now that, without understanding it, I set out in life to try to make everyone love me by trying to become anything and everything they wanted me to be. Somehow I didn't have a right to exist for myself. I had to justify my existence by making everyone around me happy and pleased with my behavior. I was like a dainty China doll. Everyone wanted to look at me, but no one seemed to care what I was really feeling inside. I don't blame them, though, because I didn't want to look inside either.

As a seventeen-year-old I chose the type of husband (a very predictable choice from what I now know) who was dominating and opinionated—just like Dad. In over twenty years of marriage he never once asked me what I needed in order to be fulfilled. Instead he only made demand after demand. And, like the unbalanced personality that I was, I tried to please him in every way and never to think of myself. But, like with my dad, my everything was never quite enough. If anything went wrong it was always my fault. Can you imagine living with overwhelming feelings of guilt and inferiority for over twenty years of married life?

As the children grew up they took on their father's role, each shackling me with new burdens, requests, and demands. No one ever asked me what I needed or wanted.

And I played right into it, feeling that it was my God-fearing duty to place my family ahead of myself. I needed their approval so much! But they never gave me their approval—just new demands.

I suppose I would have eventually died in that predicament, but something happened one day. I had enough. I don't really advocate divorce, but for the hell that my husband and I lived for most of my life, I think it was the best answer. At forty years of age I divorced him and started a life of my own.

The last several years have been some of the hardest of my life, yet some of the most precious. I have had for the first time honest feelings of

Fig. 4   THE COMPLIANT PERSPECTIVE

self-respect, self-confidence, and self-love. I'm beginning to *feel* like I have a right to exist. That God made me special and irreplaceable. My perception of God has graduated from that of a stern and rejecting Heavenly Father to a loving and empathetic Creator and Companion.

In fact, for the first time in my life, I am actually building relationships that are *mutual*, that take my needs into account too. And the guilt is gone. The only word I can think of to describe what happens when there is a balance of power and respect in a relationship is *joy*.

Sometimes I feel frustrated because it seems like I have so far to go, and because so much of my life passed by in being a partial person. But on the other hand, the progress I'm making is truly gratifying, and I thank God every day for that very precious progress.

The Compliant Perspective often begins in childhood when you learn that you win your parents' approval through pleasing and placating, and get their disapproval from assertion and self-expression. Because of this dynamic, you quickly learn to filter out your own needs and desires, and to give almost exclusive attention to what is expected from you by other people.

Such an approach mistakes getting the approval of others for being loved. This is why we say that you get stuck on the Love polarity, with compliance, pleasing and placating as your major ways of interacting with people, and as the dominant traits in your personality.

Let's go deeper into the Compliant Perspective by seeing how getting stuck and stagnant in this partial perspective can bring the personality to the brink of despair and secret depression. (As we mentioned, the *DSM III* encompasses this perspective in the Histrionic and Dependent personalities):

1. Compliant people turn to others for protection and the rewards of life. They are compelled to place their own center of gravity in other people because of an intense need for affection and attention. They require constant approval and acceptance, and become immediately distraught if this is lacking. Because they are so dependent on others, Histrionics develop a "theatrical" or deliberate display of emotion, a sort of superb sensitivity to the moods and thoughts of those they wish to please.

2. This extreme other-directedness, however, results in a life-style that is fickle and coy in patterns of behavior and emotion. Also, rather than trust themselves to one particular person for self-validation, they often master seductive and dramatic ways of getting, and trying to hold the spotlight from many people. In the Compliant Perspective, one desperately needs others to tell him or her again and again that he or she is OK. And if they do not, one rather quickly feels ill at ease and confused.

3. Usually these individuals show little interest in intellectual achievement or careful thinking. Instead, they are easily influenced by others or by fads, and often respond to any strong figure of authority who they think can provide a magical solution to their problems. Flights into romantic fantasy and wishful daydreaming are common and characterized by the idea that a knight in white armor or a loving prince will see their worth and dedicate himself to protect and adore them. But their own flightiness, vanity, attention craving, and unreliability make this fantasy unrealistic—unless they latch onto a particularly naive and needy white knight. We are emphasizing the way that women are trapped in this particular perspective because Western culture and religion seem to push it onto females. If you are a male characterized by this pattern, then the basic dynamics still apply. But boys and men tend to lean toward the Critical and Striving Perspectives, while the Compliant

and Avoidant are generally girls and women. (This, by the way, explains a great deal of what lies behind the centuries-old battle of the sexes, but that would be another book.)

4. Just to cast the Compliant Perspective onto the male, we include a quote from Carl Jung (*Psychologische Typen*, Zurich: Rascher, 1921): In the male role,

There is a marked dependence on external situations . . . anything new in the making. Because he is always seeking out new possibilities, stable conditions suffocate him. He seizes on new objects or situations with great intensity . . . only to abandon them cold-bloodedly, without any compunction . . . as soon as their range is known.

5. The Compliant personality never frees itself from its fixation at the infantile level, but remains dependent. The person affected cannot attain actuality as a mature human being, but is forced to live out a confused interplay of fantasy and reality.

6. Wilhelm Reich wrote of this partial perspective: "We find fickleness of reactions, i.e., a tendency to change one's attitudes unexpectedly and unintentionally; a strong suggestibility, which never appears alone but is coupled with a strong tendency to reactions of disappointment. An attitude of compliance is usually followed by its opposite, swift deprecation and groundless disparagement" (*Character Analysis* [3rd ed.] New York: Farrar, Straus, and Giroux, 1949, p. 205).

7. An example from the Bible of the Compliant dynamics can be seen in Martha's encounter with Jesus:

Now it came to pass, as they went, that he entered into a certain village: and a certain woman named Martha received him into her house. And she had a sister called Mary, which also sat at Jesus' feet, and heard his word. But Martha was cumbered about much serving, and came to him, and said, Lord, dost thou not care that my sister hath left me to serve alone? bid her therefore that she help me. And Jesus answered and said unto her, Martha, Martha, thou art careful and troubled about many things: But one thing is needful: and Mary hath chosen that good part, which shall not be taken away from her." (Luke 10:38-42 *KJV*)

Mary chose to encounter Jesus. Martha chose to impress him. Mary chose to let Jesus relax and be himself, and she put that choice into motion by relaxing herself and listening to what he had to say. Martha was uncomfortable and anxious about being—afraid somehow that without a wonderful performance she would not be acceptable. She flurried about and flustered herself, needlessly working and getting attention. We cannot blame her, but we can learn from Jesus' response, that it was OK to quiet herself, to gather in all her histrionic thoughts, no longer compelled to seek his approval, but content to relax and be her real self.

8. Histrionic "acting" or "performing" is directed toward an audience. It is an attempt to hypnotize others into participating in the fantasy that the Histrionic person's life is bigger and more wonderful than it really is. Since "success" depends largely on how one is marketed, there is an anxious inner pressure to sell the personality through exaggerated excitement and dramatization. But such people's feelings of identity become as shaky as their self-esteem; their identity is constituted by the sum total of roles they can play: "I am as you desire me."

9. Perhaps the most colorful description of the Compliant and Histrionic personality is that it is "emotionally labile, irresponsible, shallow, love-intoxicated, giddy and short-sighted . . . possessive, grasping, demanding, romantic. . . . When frustrated or disappointed, reproachful, tearful, abusive, and vindictive. . . . Rejection sensitivity is perhaps their outstanding com-

mon clinical feature" (D. F. Klein, *Psychiatric Case Studies,* Baltimore: Williams and Wilkins, 1972, p. 237).

If you discover yourself in this description, then how do you go about changing? Well, it is not as hard as you might think, especially if you are sick and tired of living for other people's praise or approval. If you desperately need somebody's approval, you make them your judge and jury. You must tirelessly convince them how good you are, or they will quickly find some single shortcoming and convict you of the charge of not meeting their expectations.

But why should you exist to meet someone else's expectations? Especially since all humans are created equal in their ability to be foolish. Why not trust your own judgment for a change, and do what seems best to you? Is your own judgment that much worse than the next person's, or than the particular, fallible person whom you make into a god?

We challenge you to dare to quit sacrificing your genuine identity at the altar of someone else's ego, no matter how cocksure, pious, religious, powerful, or utterly charming they may be. Give yourself a break. Quit looking to your audience and begin to be your true self in earnest. And do not just blindly live it. Choose it day to day, hour to hour. Create, with God's assistance, the person you are called to be. And do not lay all kinds of expectations and demands upon God. Chances are he wants you just to relax, and then to go from there, to break out of that vicious circle of performing and trying to be something great in order to win his approval and attention. You already have both, so just relax and see what happens next.

To change and grow toward wholeness, the Compliant person needs to be made more assertive and strong. A new synthesis results from integrating the qualities of Assertion and Strength. This process is described by Charlotte Clinebell in her book, *Meet Me in the Middle* (1973, pp. 3-4):

Lately I've come to understand one reason that Mother's Day has always bothered me either vaguely or violently: I never felt I measured up to the "Holy, Holy, Holy" image it demands. Although I never let myself think such a thought then, I believe I had a sneaking suspicion that I didn't really want to be so selfless and perfect. Although I strove to be devout and sweet and lighthearted, and loyal and compliant and sensitive, and though I succeeded at some of those things some of the time, mostly I did not. I was often angry, often raised my voice at my husband or children, often was sulky or martyred or blue . . . . Furthermore, my family was not always happy. Whether or not I *was* responsible for their unhappiness, I *felt* responsible. The ideal woman keeps her family happy and successful. What an impossible burden to bear! . . . It's true that there is a part of me that is tender and sweet (maybe even delicate!) and spiritual and sympathetic and compliant and dependent and unselfish and compassionate and nurturing and serving and anxious to please and be liked. But now I know that there's a very real part of me that is assertive and aggressive and self-seeking and strong and competent and intelligent and achieving. If only I had been able to use *that* side of me more fully instead of feeling guilty about it, I would have been a happier human being and a more honest one. Now I'm discovering it's not too late.

According to our overview of the LAWS of personality, the victim of the Compliant Perspective is overly committed to the Love polarity in dealing with life. This leaves such a person overly sweet and nice, and means that that person is deficient in skills pertaining to the Assertion polarity.

Growing numbers of psychologists and theologians now regard assertion simply as an active effort on the part of a person to cope with the difficulties of life through:

* honesty

* self-expressiveness

* direct and firm decision making
* self-enhancing and socially responsible actions
* questioning when in doubt or insufficient information has been provided
* saying no to things one truly does not believe or does not choose to do
* refusing to feel guilt when, in one's best judgment, the situation does not genuinely call for it
* standing up for one's reasonable right to disagree, take a contrary stand, or negotiate with anyone
* cherishing one's autonomy, while still being open to the Holy Spirit within, or the inputs of others from without.

We like the definition of assertion provided by Alberti and Emmons in *Your Perfect Right* (1982, p. 3):

Assertive behavior enables a person to act in his or her own best interests, to stand up for herself or himself without undue anxiety, to express honest feelings comfortably, or to exercise personal rights without denying the rights of others.

There is no single way to handle all situations with the proper balance of love and assertion, other than the way Jesus himself lived on earth. So rather than waiting forever to learn these skills, you must instead learn them through practicing again and again in your own behavior. For now, accept the great importance that both polarities, Love and Assertion, are vital to healthy psychological and spiritual functioning. Then take it from there with your own creative attempts to integrate these mutually interfacing opposites.

The only real caution we wish to give is that you need to be careful not to harbor too much anger or resentment in your assertion. Paul makes a superb point when he writes: "If you are angry, don't sin by nursing your grudge. Don't let the sun go down with you still angry—get over it quickly" (Ephesians 4:26 *TLB*). The emotion we call anger involves a dramatic rise in the amount of adrenalin released into the bloodstream. God built that adrenalin-releasing mechanism into our bodies so that we could feel aroused if something unjust, life-threatening, or simply exploitative and manipulative were to happen. The quick burst of that same chemical in Jesus' body aroused him to assert himself along a whole continuum of ways, from direct and firm speech (to the Pharisees or in regard to his view of Herod) to strong physical arousal (as when he expelled the money changers from the Temple). Between these extremes there were many times when he challenged, rebuked, corrected, or confounded those closest to him, the twelve disciples.

With healthy assertiveness the point is to get it over quickly, to express the little irritations and annoyances as close to the time of origin as possible. Holding in angry feelings for indefinite periods of time or just plain being afraid to speak up for yourself are the real dangers here, because they allow the ill-feeling or discontent to remain hidden and unresolved.

We will say much more about the healthy expression of irritation or annoyance in the chapter on the Critical Perspective, because those who lose contact with love within the personality, and only thrive on anger, become the opposite of compliant people—they become anger-dominated. The *DSM III* calls them the Paranoid and Antisocial personalities.

This fact of personality underscores our central thesis, that truth is not found in extreme expressions or rigid control. Rather, the truth of healthy and Spirit-filled Christian personalities occurs in the synthesis of the Spirit and individual person; a "putting together" into a more creative whole the rhythmic expressions of Love and Assertion, Weakness and Strength that each unique moment of life calls for.

EXERCISES

1. Can you learn to want to see yourself more clearly? Can you develop the courage to not be tearfully defensive, but to honestly desire to understand your own personality in terms of our LAWS? Can you accept our premise that "the facts are friendly"? Think and pray about your desire to see things as they really are, instead of trying only to be secure in perhaps a phoney or immature perception.

2. Spend a little time each day committing figure 3, "Overview of 'Stuckness' vs. Growth" to memory. A picture is worth a thousand words, and a map of human personality and relationships is worth forty or fifty years of hit-or-miss, trial and error learning.

3. If your personality is too shaped by the Compliant Perspective, pray specifically that God will give you opportunities to be more open, more assertive. Decide in your heart to face hidden fears about possible rejection, and start learning to believe in yourself more.

4. Watch carefully the behavior of those around you who can diplomatically express themselves without hiding or compromising too much. Begin to internalize such models by seeing yourself acting the same way, and try the new behavior out for yourself. Before long you will have learned skills that will become indigenous and spontaneous to your own personality.

7

THE CRITICAL PERSPECTIVE
(ASSERTION POLARITY)

Don't criticize, and then you won't be criticized. For others will treat you as you treat them. And why worry about a speck in the eye of a brother when you have a board in your own?

—Jesus Christ

The most frightening person to deal with in the world is the person who functions first and foremost from the Critical Perspective, unless you are that person. This is because the individual caught in the Critical Perspective uses many of his or her energies to dominate, blame, attack, discredit, slander, interrogate, scorn, shun, reproach, condemn, investigate, backbite, derogate, disapprove of, or just plain be fickle and contrary to others.

We suppose it is no accident that the Bible nicknames Satan "the accuser of our brethren" (Revelation 12:10 KJV). To be jealous over someone's good fortune, to be offended by someone's gifts or strengths, to despise someone's sincere achievements are devilish things to do. And do not think for a moment that the devil is the only one who acts this way. We all blame and attack to some extent, even if we seem to be sweet and innocent. It's part of our human limitations, our fallen human nature, to feel downright jealous, envious, or upset now and then at someone else's blessing. And normally we become aware

Fig. 5   THE CRITICAL PERSPECTIVE

of the negative feeling, ask God to help us get over it quickly, and move ahead to improve or accept our own lot.

But the person stuck in the Critical Perspective—who cannot and will not swing back into love and caring—functions chronically from that limited perspective. And what we do most often, we become proficient at (see figure 5).

The best single adjective to describe the person caught in the spell of the Critical Perspective is *sadistic*. And we have in mind no sexual connotation, although that can certainly occur. What we mean is an unusual delight, a kind of private pleasure in being cruel to another person. The sadistic personality (called by the *DSM III* the Paranoid or Antisocial personality) plays the game of life by rules that totally astound and perplex other people. That is because the person affected places his or her self above all rules except the rule of getting even, of being on top, of making others somehow and in some ingenious way that person's debtors and slaves.

It took America precious, irreplaceable years to take sides in World War II, simply because we could not conceive of, would not dare to believe in, a paranoid quality such as Hitler's. But it was there, alive and in bloody color, a fact of life. The longer we waited and made excuses, the more costly became the ultimate sacrifice required to turn back Hitler's paranoia. And it is always the same when we allow a Paranoid personality to invade and then take over our lives. The longer we wait to take strong retaliatory stands, the more exacting the price we pay to escape the bondage and to rediscover and reaffirm our freedom.

Common parlance has it that paranoia means being overly suspicious and feeling that one is being somehow plotted against. This interpretation misses a deeper attribute of paranoia—namely, that one feels it is right and just to use any means at one's disposal to control people—and the best way is always to create fear and self-doubt in them.

To deepen your understanding of this most perplexing and devastating (to others) of our four partial perspectives, we draw from some *DSM III* descriptions of the Paranoid personality:

1. It must always win at all costs, and if it does not, you somehow sense it will not be at rest until victory comes.

2. It immediately discounts and discards as stupid or useless any point of view other than its own.

Author's personal comment—Dan:

Close to fifteen years ago I began meeting with a group of Protestant professors at a college where I taught. In the group were an equal number of Catholic priests. The dialogue had been going on for two years prior to my attending the session I am about to describe.

What had originated the group meetings, which most individuals characterized as being provocative, keen, insightful, and exciting, was a desire to breach a centuries-old gap between these two major traditions of the Christian faith. I was all for it.

Over dozens of months, carefully prepared and diplomatically worded presentations had been given by both groups on such subjects of mutual interest as the nature of salvation, the role of the Holy Spirit in the believer's life, the respective roles of the dialectic between the authority of the Bible, the authority of the believer, and the authority of tradition, and more.

During my second session, I had been much stimulated but was too shy to speak. The site was a large Catholic church in the Middle West, and the topic was the role of the Holy Spirit in a Christian's life.

There was an electric feeling because the two newest guests included both the bishop of the diocese and the pastor of the largest Protestant church in the state, a church numbering over two thousand people.

After a delightful lunch prepared by the sisters, the bishop spoke first, and made sensitive and intriguing comments that fostered our sense of mutual exploration into the topic at hand.

Then all eyes turned to the Protestant minister.

He stood up, adjusted his glasses, grasped his Bible firmly in hand, and announced: "If you Catholics are finally ready to admit that the Holy Bible is the only authoritative revelation of God to the human race, and if you are ready right now to receive Jesus Christ as your personal Savior, then we have something to talk about. If not, then I don't see any point to staying any longer!"

An icy silence thicker than fog covered the room. I shuddered. We were speechless.

Then he walked out.

As I've reflected on this experience over the years, I realize that here was not an evil man, just a man who had no self-correcting balances within his personality. He was doing the best he could, and certainly thought he was making a great stand in behalf of the Bible and Jesus. It's just that the blind spots in his personality compelled him to focus on everyone else's problems and not his own. And being stuck on the Assertion polarity made it difficult and sometimes even impossible to get in touch with another person's feelings or point of view. Without empathy and openness, he left the meeting with the illusion that he had single-handedly blitzkrieged the damnable Catholics and scored a mighty victory for God.

3. The Paranoid personality makes "mountains out of molehills" by way of senseless argumentation, and finds it very difficult ever to really relax because it carries so much inner tension.

4. It is extremely rigid in thought and is unwilling to compromise.

5. It intimidates others regularly, generating uneasiness and fear, but it has great difficulty seeing its own mistakes or weaknesses. It resents loudly and flies into counterattacks if anyone insinuates that it too has faults or biases.

6. It takes great pride in being always logical, objective, and rational. And it would deny the charge if someone suggested it was seldom tender, compassionate, or merciful. It does experience these softer feelings, but usually only within the larger predominant pattern of using these feelings to influence and seduce people—as Hitler did when he had public relations films made of him holding and humming to little children. The bottom line is always power and control, not love or respect.

7. It is moralistic when this suits, grandiose regularly, and adept at feigning humility or shyness when this advances a cause.

8. It considers itself a hard-headed realist, smarter and superior in every way to the Compliant, Helpless, and even Narcissistic personalities it seeks to dominate and lead.

What we need to realize is that there cannot be any reign of a Paranoid or Antisocial person without the willing submission of loyal and obedient servants. It is not entirely the Paranoid's fault that others cower under his or her regime. It is a shared bondage, a mutual interlocking of traits that can operate on any level, superficial or intimate.

One or both parents can have paranoid tendencies. Uncles, grandparents, siblings—even best friends—can have their personalities taken over by these compulsions. Your job, if you are the Paranoid, is to forego the exercise of your power as a mechanism of control and to learn to utilize this power in ways that express your love for the people close to you. If you are the victim of a Paranoid personality, a grasshopper caught in the web of a black widow, it is your task, with the assistance of God and insight, to extricate yourself, and leave the spider to contemplate its behavior alone.

Rarely can an untrained person turn around the ways of a Paranoid. It usually takes extreme professional skill to do so. That is why we say to get out; to leave that situation. Make a new life, taking with you the learning you paid years or months of humiliation to acquire. Your experience will serve you well in the future, and God will be with you.

Are Paranoid and Antisocial tendencies unchangeable? Is one who is stuck on the Assertion polarity in the Critical Perspective beyond redemption? Heavens no. Nobody is beyond redemption. No partial personality is beyond the love of God, or beyond the power of the Holy Spirit to penetrate, heal, and inspire. But before we get into that process of growth and healing, we want to mention one more awesome characteristic of the people who live out of the Critical Perspective.

They love to prick bubbles. They enjoy putting a needle through your enjoyment of anything. First they make you some kind of underdog who always needs their OK or approval. That means they train you to report everything to them. Then they always inform you that what you did was wrong, how you acted was inappropriate, how you felt was unreal, and what you learned was stupid.

The Paranoid personality is a huge magnetic force that makes your own inner gyroscope go crazy in its presence—even though you may live a thousand miles away and what you said was through a letter or phone call.

Start noticing the knot in your stomach, the constriction of your throat, the constipation or diarrhea that follows the encounter, the tightness in your chest. These are all God-given symptoms to alert you that you are being held captive! You are not free to be who you are; you are not free to fulfill your mission and calling; you are not free to relax and follow the gentle inner promptings of the Holy Spirit—you are a slave to another fallible human being's whim! And that fact alone should catapult you out of his or her orbit and into God's guidance. However mysterious you have heard God's ways can be, he is not sadistic, stern, merciless, egocentric, or insatiably dictatorial. Is he? You have to determine the answer to this question in your own mind and heart, because the real controlling Paranoid will do everything in his or her power to keep even God under control. They often believe they speak on God's behalf, even using select Bible verses handily.

Once you have diagnosed that you are the victim of a powerful Paranoid personality, then go ahead and rebel—little by little, if that will do the job, or all at once, if that is what it takes.

It is rather sad that Christianity as a whole seems to attach such negativism to rebellion. Rebellion is the most sensible and constructive alternative to a depersonalizing dilemma—the very predicament that Paranoid personalities create for everyone within their sphere of influence.

Gayle Erwin writes, in *The Jesus Style:*

A particular characteristic of manipulation is that it destroys our ability to choose. It forces us to move defensively into the pattern or mold that others have chosen for us. Not a single person who tried to manipulate Jesus got the answer they expected. All of them received an expression of the true feelings of Jesus. From some of them he withdrew. In each case he protected his ability to choose.

There is a distinctive difference between coerced slavery and servanthood by choice. When Jesus stated that he chose to lay down his life and that no one was taking it from him, he was describing the basic element of love. . . . True love cannot be the result of either decree, force or manipulation. Anything that I do to deprive someone of the right to choose is a violation of his personhood. When I sense that my own right to choose is being threatened, then I know that I am not being loved. (1983, p. 51)

Perhaps the rebel, then, has a spark of God in his or her heart, a passion for what he or she can be in their soul. To rebel is to question with deep intent; for someone who has been hypnotized by a Paranoid—whether by country, employer, or spouse—that questioning is the right and privilege of a person who wishes to be a participant with self respect . . . not a faceless slave.

The second thing to notice if you are held captive by a Paranoid is that Paranoids are haunted by a possessive jealousy and they use it to torture and torment. This is because keeping a hold over the victim is of more absorbing interest to them than their own lives. This *is* their lives: to have satellites buzzing all around; to have the most people in their orbit for the least possible effort, let alone positive affirmation. They need to own you— heart, body, mind, spirit, and soul. Anything short of this arouses their indignation, or causes them to pout or withdraw. The sucking nature of the Paranoid's agenda needs to be emphasized and taken very seriously here.

But here is the rub. Here is the carrot ahead of the donkey, the promise that lures us on. The Paranoid will first promise you the world, and then when push comes to shove, give you just enough to keep you hooked and interested. All the more reason to master the LAWS of personality we are presenting and take strong stands, in the name of your own freedom and autonomy before God, to resist such dizzying and dazzling tactics. Yes, you need a certain amount of experience with such a person before you can even begin to discern the bottom line, but we encourage you to drop that person quickly in order to increase your own growth and self-realization. You do not need a Paranoid's crumbs of approval, and that is all you will ever get. Let him or her be, and move on with your own life mission. Do not try to convince the Paranoid, because he or she will only refute and argue with you. Just go. And grow. And transcend the Assertion pole that such people are stuck under by integrating love, compassion, empathy, and the genuine letting go of others that you long for and need for yourself.

Remember that the chief motivation of the Paranoid, the person with the Critical Perspective, is to exploit others; what matters most is getting the better of others. Therefore they regularly subject their unconsciously obliging underdogs, directly or indirectly, to ever mounting demands, and still make the subservient feel guilty or humiliated or helpless if they do not fulfill these demands. And besides getting immense pleasure out of making others feel lower than a snake's navel, they also derive great satisfaction from poisoning people's joy and disappointing their expectations. Any satisfaction or emotional excitement on the part of others almost irresistibly provokes them to spoil it in some way. How else can they keep their underdogs from growing beyond their sphere of influence? How else can they keep them dependent and deprived before the altar of their phenomenally huge egos?

Perhaps a word here is appropriate to give insight into the Critical Perspective. Nobody develops intense Paranoid and Antisocial characteristics who does not experience an equal amount of painful humiliation and futility at some crucial point in his or her own development. Whatever the particular circumstances, the outcome is that he or she feels forever excluded, forever defeated.

As Karen Horney says:

His self-loathing reaches such dimensions that he cannot take a look at himself. He must fortify himself against it by reinforcing an already existing armor of righteousness. The slightest criticism, neglect, or absence of special recognition can mobilize his self-contempt . . . to blame, berate, humiliate others. . . .

He usually rationalizes the pressure he exerts on the partner as "love" or interest in the partner's "development." Needless to say, it is not love. . . . In reality he tries to enforce upon the partner the impossible task of realizing his—the sadist's—idealized image. The righteousness which he had to develop as a shield against self-contempt permits him to do so with smug assurance. (*Our Inner Conflicts*, 1945, pp. 204-5)

With compassion we can understand a Paranoid's inner struggle. The vindictiveness that seeps through every cell of his or her body like poison is turned outward in the form of violent contempt for someone else. And self-righteous insulation keeps that person from ever seeing that he or she chronically abuses and victimizes others.

And here is the secret that perpetuates this neurotic dynamic. Paranoid personalities mold the lives of others with complete justification from their own "ruined" lives, and as they mold they gain a stimulating feeling of power, a power that brings a substitute meaning to their own lives. When they exploit others emotionally, they gain vicarious emotional life for themselves that lessens their own sense of barrenness, emptiness, and futility. When they defeat others, they win a victorious elation which obscures their own hopeless defeat. This craving for vindictive triumph is probably the most intense, compeling, motivating force in their lives.

It is truly amazing to see how much paranoid behavior can be heaped upon others without their knowing it. The greater part of what Paranoids do in daily behavior is for the most part hidden from consciousness. Their numbness to feelings of their own and of others is one factor that adds to the blindness. A desperate but increasingly intense search for meaning through power over others is another. Their powers are not used to enhance and support, but to defeat and control the personalities of those around them.

With all this in mind we can now clearly recognize that the destructive mode of the Critical Perspective is undeniable. But at the same time we can understand a suffering human being who stands behind the seemingly inhuman behavior. With this overview we open the possibility of reaching such a walled off human being through therapy, through prayer, or through Spirit-inspired articulations of a former underdog's breaking the spell of the Paranoid and calling things for what they are.

What you need to realize here is that persons with the Critical Perspective, individuals who cling to the Assertive polarity to the exclusion of Love, Weakness, and actual (not presumptuous) Strength—such people may have precious little motivation for change. They are in charge, and they experience exhilaration from their power. In other words, they like the way things are, and are determined to keep them that way come hell or high water. So the courage and motivation for change must come from the oppressed, not the oppressor . . . from the accused, confused, and misused—not their keepers.

We would be remiss here if we did not draw attention to a historical and psychological fact—a fact that many Christians tend to deny: that is, that a long overdue balance between men and women is finally beginning to emerge throughout the Christian world. This means that in centuries past as well as throughout most of the twentieth century, women have been unfairly shackled in roles with functionally less power than men.

How many women do you know who are deacons or on the boards of the churches in your community? How many are included as lay ministers in the offering of communion—the Lord's Supper—to the congregation? How many are encouraged or allowed to attend seminary to become professional theologians, scholarly participants for new biblical translations, or pastors? How many are encouraged or allowed to become pastoral counselors?

Early church fathers frequently depicted women as evil temptresses, carriers of the guilt of Eve, and brainless ninnies who could be led easily astray from sound doctrine. Tertullian wrote: "Woman, you are the devil's doorway. You have led astray one whom the devil would not dare to attack directly. It is your fault that the Son of God had to die; you should always go in mourning and in rags."

But we are living in the twentieth century now, and it is becoming evident to many that inequality between the sexes is an artificial and destructive concept. When women honestly believed that they were intellectually inferior and more emotionally unstable than men, it was logical to accept a position of subservience. Now, however, in the face of modern knowledge that women are not inherently "weaker," do not (except when they freely so choose) "belong" only in the home, and can indeed make invaluable and crucial contributions to every single facet of life, it is much more difficult to build a closed case for keeping women in their old places.

But the ingenious answer found by many of today's Christian laymen and clergy (male, of course) is that men and women are "equal . . . just different." The difference, of course, despite the eloquent rhetoric, amounts to keeping Christian women economically dependent, intellectually intimidated, and generally restricted to affairs of home and children.

We call this situation a classic example of top dog vs. underdog in a power structure that puts the man on top, because he is somehow mysteriously closer to God and therefore keener and more discerning.

As you will see by referring to figure 1 on page 31, full-blown male top dogs literally dominate their underdog counterparts because they take over the two upper polarities, Assertion and Strength. The two bottom polarities, Weakness and Love, are naturally relegated to the underdogs, women. Such an arbitrary and unfair splitting of what should constitute every whole Christian personality, whether male or female, is a crime.

Let us ask you, as a parent: do you want your little daughter to grow up feeling somehow less capable, more limited, and carefully consigned to becoming weak, subservient, and dependent on either her sibling brothers or your neighbor's boy kid? Do you want her to grow up into a sweet, obedient, full-blown partial personality—who attracts men like a magnet and then marries and lives miserably ever after with her psychological opposite—a Paranoid and Narcissistic man?

It seems to us that the age-old battle of the sexes, whether in the church or culture at large, can be pretty much eradicated by giving each child, without sexual discrimination, equal training in the art and skills of Love, Assertion, Weakness, and Strength. These kinds of children—children who themselves possess whole personalities—draw and attract equally healthy partners. And the goal of their relationship will remain mutual growth and development of the deepest and highest calling in each.

It is a marvelous tribute to the apostle Paul that he was inspired to write: "For as many of you as have been baptized into Christ have put on Christ. . . . there is neither bond nor free, there is neither male nor female: for ye are all one in Christ Jesus" (Galatians 3:27, 28 *KJV*).

In the last analysis, all spiritual shortcomings, neurotic conflicts, personality disorders, and partial perspectives can be used for good or evil—for redemption and healing, or for self-defeating aims. But the Christian who is growing in the Lord accepts these limitations as invitations to experience the grace of God and the humble knowledge of one's need for continued guidance and purification through the intimate presence of the Holy Spirit within.

EXERCISES

1. Which are you—a top dog or underdog? Admit your answer openly to God and to yourself.

2. Do you use guilt constructively or destructively in your life? The most guilt you should ever feel should last only ten minutes or so. Then act on the guilt in a constructive way by confessing your fault to God, and attempting to rectify the situation, to make retribution for the offense, or to apologize for your error. Guilt lasting beyond this can become very neurotic and very unproductive for you or anybody else. When you feel guilt, weigh it, pray about it, and then deal with it, either through realizing that the guilt is in fact a false and unproductive feeling (a "should" laid on you by someone else), or that it is authentic and therefore should be acted upon through positive measures immediately. If the guilt is too confusing and persistent to wade through, then open up to a trusted friend or seek the clarification of a professional counselor or psychologist.

3. If you are a person with the Critical Perspective, do a little psychological archeology to determine in your own mind how this came about. If you can, get important information about how you were brought up, how your parents interacted with you and themselves, and how any of your brothers or sisters might fit into the picture. How did you come to take the position that moving against others through aggression, intimidation, and faultfinding was the best way to live? Declare inwardly to God your desire and determination to become more balanced . . . more open, empathetic, and sensitive to others. Watch for the new ways in which people begin to respond to you

when you use your sense of personal power to help them instead of hurt them, to bless them instead of burden them, to give them emotional security instead of undermine their sense of identity.

4. Generally, the person with the Compliant Perspective has too much guilt and too little anger, while the opposite, the person with the Critical Perspective, has too little guilt and too much anger. If you are a Critical person, you need to feel guilt more often and hold back your anger more often. Only then can you begin to see how isolated in your little psychological machine-gun turret you have become. Start taking seriously the comments that others have been making about you for years. They have seen clearly how you use anger, fear, and guilt to intimidate and control. They have also noticed that you never listen to constructive criticism, and that you have an answer for everything. Listen to them! They are trying to find a way to break through your shell. Make friends with anxiety because you are going to have to experience your share in order for any real personal growth to occur. We challenge you to do this, and to see if the change you gradually experience within and in how people perceive you is not worth a thousandfold the effort you make.

8

THE HELPLESS PERSPECTIVE
(WEAKNESS POLARITY)

You must be brave enough to understand yourself, wise enough to see your potentials, and courageous enough to work and play with God to make them real.

—Dan Montgomery

Human beings have a deep, instinctive need to be loved and affirmed. When we are not respected, and are discounted instead, we experience worry, doubt, rebellion, withdrawal, hurt, or fear. Of all these emotional negatives, perhaps the most universal is fear. Fear is built into human existence. We must all learn to cope with it. Psychoanalyst Karen Horney has emphasized the disabling power of fear by her term basic anxiety, which we define as free-floating fear:

Through a variety of adverse influences, a child may not be permitted to grow according to his individual needs and possibilities. . . . As a result, the child does not develop a feeling of belonging. . . . but instead a profound insecurity and vague apprehensiveness. The cramping pressure of his basic anxiety prevents the child from relating himself to others with the spontaneity of his real feelings. (*Our Inner Conflicts*)

We have learned in years of counseling that we all become afraid in life. We are all in the same boat when it comes to fear. It is just that some people are better at covering it up than others. Here are some of the fears we experience either consciously or unconsciously:

* fear of failure
* fear of disapproval or rejection
* fear of losing health, money, prestige, or livelihood
* fear of the unknown
* fear of self-discovery and self-disclosure
* fear of God or fear of the devil
* fear of responsibility
* fear of growing up
* fear of growing old
* fear of dying
* fear of the economy
* fear of invasion by a foreign power
* fear of being victim to violent crime
* and, yes, believe it or not, fear of happiness, which we call "happiness anxiety"

Once, during an evening of group therapy with ten participants, a top business executive expressed the fear that he was going to become an alcoholic under the pressure of work, a pastor shared that he had never worked through a pervasive fear of people, a wife confessed that she felt terrified about her sexual attraction to another man, a parent spoke of feeling fearful about how a teenage son was rebelling, and an artist told of fear that she could never paint a great picture again.

Being a Christian does not mean that we no longer feel afraid. It means that we have Someone to take our fears to and share them with. As Billy Graham says, being born again does not mean that "we will never have any problems." We will, "but we do have Someone to help us face our problems. The Christian life is not a way 'out' but a way 'through' life."

Often, it only takes the courage to tell our fears to someone who can accept and understand us, and the fears will melt into a new and more positive feeling. On the night of which we just spoke, because of the warm interpersonal climate of the therapy group, every person who discussed his or her fear left feeling relieved and encouraged. It is no accident that James writes, "Confess your faults one to another, and pray one for another, that ye may be healed" (James 5:16 KJV).

The person who functions from the Helpless Perspective lives in the grip of fear for years, and sometimes, if the fear remains unresolved, for a lifetime.

Author's personal comment—Dan:

I will never forget what a woman of sixty said in a church group I was leading over ten years ago. She and her husband had been missionaries to China for over thirty-five years, and had started several dozen Christian churches in their lifetime together. They had tirelessly loved and educated peasants in numerous villages. Hundreds of sincere people had returned her gift of love, especially for bringing them the gospel, and Christ's personal love for each one of them.

But she could never take in deeply their love. And in spite of preaching several thousand messages about God's profound and all-encompassing love, she herself felt a secret distance from her Creator and Redeemer. In tears—the most she had cried in years—she confessed to us that ever since early childhood days she had felt somehow unacceptable to God. She knew intellectually she was "saved," but emotionally she felt distant and alone.

What could account for such a tragic discrepancy? She was stuck in the Helpless Perspective. But because she had never learned how human personalities are shaped and formed, and how they can change and grow, she remained stuck for most of a lifetime. Fortunately, God blesses us no matter what our feelings or weaknesses. We can praise God and admire Sister Maurine precisely because she accomplished so very much even in the context of hidden inferiority feelings.

All of us need to realize that just giving in to feelings of helplessness doesn't accomplish anything. But if we utilize the feelings to rely on God to strengthen and help us, he will, and we can accomplish quite a lot in regard to our individual callings. Also, some of us are natural introverts—more sensitive and reflective in nature. That is OK, but being hampered by unnecessary fear is not OK.

I am thrilled to tell you now that in the next several group sessions, Sister Maurine, as she liked to be called, worked through her fears. They melted into feelings of relaxation and self-acceptance, and most of all, a triumphant discovery of feeling loved by God.

It turned out that neither of her parents had ever hugged or loved her as a child. They didn't know how to give physical or even verbal love. So when she gave her heart to her Heavenly Father at the age of eight, she unconsciously expected the same emotional distance. That unconscious, irrational, rigid expectation dominated her life and personality until the age of sixty, when she finally learned how to seek it from the Holy Spirit within and from the group. Now her feelings happily and strongly support her theology about God's love. And now you can see that love in the beaming countenance of her face.

The Christian with the Helpless Perspective is in the same boat with the rest of us when it comes to having weaknesses. The only difference is that he or she is stuck on the Weakness polarity, so that the feeling of weakness becomes chronic. Self-consciousness is a way of life. Embarrassment comes easy. There is a lot of shyness and little sense of personal right to life, liberty, and the pursuit

Fig. 6   THE HELPLESS PERSPECTIVE

of happiness. There is no Strength polarity experience to balance out the Weakness (see figure 6).

Christian psychiatrist Paul Tournier writes of the Helpless Perspective:

Neurosis, shyness, feelings of inferiority, lack of self-confidence, hypersensitivity, pathological feelings of guilt, emotional instability, obsessions, panic, functional disturbances, indecision, and depression are the expression of weak reactions. In their turn, all these unhealthy manifestations maintain in the subject a feeling of weakness which provokes him to further weak reactions. (*The Strong and the Weak*, p. 27)

Such people are hyperconscious of their weakness because they have never felt love. They have the appearance of being ill, failures, and overwhelmed by life. The weak allow themselves to be crushed because they believe in the strength of the "strong" (those caught in the Striving, Critical, and Compliant Perspectives) but cannot believe in their own strength and potential. They are abiding by only one of the LAWS of personality, while remaining out of synchronization with the other three.

In the terms of the *DSM III*, the Helpless Perspective, if rigid enough, can take on the personality configuration diagnosed clinically as the Avoidant or Schizoid personality.

To enable you to identify yourself or someone you care for who may be functioning out of the Helpless Perspective, here is a more composite picture of this partial personality (Not everyone, of course, will have all these characteristics):

1. They are oversensitive to the moods and feelings of others. Their extreme fear of rejection or humiliation intrudes into their thoughts, and causes them to actively distance themselves from others to guard against the psychological pain they anticipate.

2. They withdraw from opportunities for developing

love or close relationships because of a fearful expectation of being belittled or put down. Equally distant is their relationship with God—even though they cognitively accept him into their lives, they strongly doubt his genuine love at an emotional level. They seesaw between hoping he loves them, and somehow feeling certain that when the chips are down, he does not.

3. Depression, free-floating anxiety, and anger at themselves for failing to develop social relations are commonly present.

4. There is constant, frenetic self-analysis and comparison: "How am I impressing people? What do they think of me? What have I done wrong now? How can I ever make it through life?" About God they think, "He could never love me if he knew what I am really like."

5. Qualities of shyness, nervousness, timidity, distrustfulness, and hypersensitivity cause them to often feel like a basket case of "nerves."

6. They are so preoccupied with fears and insecurities that they constantly imagine they are in danger, and therefore always pursue the course of greatest safety. The desperate desire to feel safe is a compelling motivator of behavior.

7. What is crucial is their inner need to put distance between themselves and others by drawing around themselves a kind of magic circle that no one may penetrate.

8. Their goals are negative: not to be involved, not to need anyone, not to allow others to intrude on, influence, or emotionally bond to them.

9. With little or no real evidence, they conclude within their own minds that others look down on them, do not take them seriously, and do not care for their company.

10. Desires for affection may be strong, but these are self-protectively denied, repressed, or restrained. They deeply fear placing their need or welfare in the hands of

others. Their need for human affection is usually displaced, and may pour forth in poetry or sensitively detailed artistic creations, in caring tenderly for animals, or in intellectual pursuits.

11. Most people who have contact with Avoidant personalities tend to see them as timid, or perhaps distant or eccentric. Those who relate to them more closely, however, quickly discover their underlying sensitivities, along with their elusiveness, touchiness, moodiness, and pervasive apprehension.

12. Avoidants describe themselves as fearful, ill at ease, and sad. They voice futility in regard to the life they lead, have a deflated self-image, and frequently refer to themselves with an attitude of contempt or derision.

13. Every route toward gratification or fulfillment seems blocked by conflicts. They cannot act on their own because of marked self-doubt; at the same time they cannot depend on others because of mistrust. They are trapped in the worst of both worlds, seeking to avoid the distress that surrounds them and the emptiness and hurts that gnaw away within them.

14. Repression of all feelings seems the only thing to do. This accounts for the Avoidant's initial appearance of being emotionally flat, physically pale, socially indifferent, and spiritually stilted. The appearance, to the trained eye, gives away the torturous inner turmoil and intense buried feelings that these people truly experience.

15. Even with their full defenses intact, these individuals still characteristically seem on edge, unable to relax, worrisome, easily startled, irritable, preoccupied with calamities, and prone to insomnia or nightmares. They also suffer inexplicable fatigue, and usually have poor appetites.

As you can see from this personality profile, fear is a harsh taskmaster, and extracts a severe toll from the person who is captive to the Helpless Perspective.

To enhance our empathy and compassion for such people, we need only recognize how self-defeating their behaviors are. They are resistant to growth or change, and cling to even the most obviously self-denying routines simply because these do not require a new choice. They cannot explore alternative actions without feeling intense anxiety.

Rather than venturing outward or drawing upon what aptitudes they do indeed possess, they retreat defensively and become increasingly remote from others and removed from sources and opportunities for potential growth.

For all of us, the ability to change often goes in waves—a back and forth movement of venturing out to a new way of operating, but then finding ourselves retreating to old patterns. Acknowledging our ambivalence and even downright resistance to growth can be healthy. But we cannot afford to just walk off the field of life and not try to cope anymore. We will only become weaker and more avoidant.

Avoidants seem compelled by inner fears to settle for a very modest level of comfort by detaching themselves from others and taking no further risks. They prefer to let matters stand, keep to the level of adjustment to which they are accustomed (no matter how sterile, isolated, or dehumanized), and not rock the boat that they have so tenaciously learned to sail.

In regard to relating to God, these individuals prefer a more distant, passive, and marginal orientation. Getting too close to a personal God brings the same inner onslaught of fear and trepidation that getting close to any person brings. Any spiritual experience that breaks into the rigidly controlled existence they have grown accustomed to is unwelcome and highly threatening.

Now whether you are rigidly Avoidant or Schizoid, or simply have a few tendencies to be, the following guidelines for breaking out of the Helpless Perspective personality style will be useful.

You can dramatically change yourself if you believe you can. If you are willing to give up the self-defeating behaviors of shyness, numbness to feelings, and fear of encounters with others, the Helpless Perspective, even the severest kind, can be curtailed. But it takes commitment.

Author's personal comment—Ev:

I feel especially empathetic toward you if your personality was cast from the shy and avoidant mold. Mine was too.

I remember as a youngster standing on an Illinois street corner as a member of a team of Salvation Army workers. I remember now I was feeling shy and avoidant. But I didn't know the terminology then. I was really afraid!

In one way my Salvation Army rearing was inspiring. The hymns we used to sing still move me deeply. In another way it brought me a sense of endurance and humility because we worked with the poor, the helpless, and the needy—the more unfortunate than I. Even so, God was presented as being a stern and demanding General, and this perception caused me pain. It made me fearful and anxious, always on the lookout for his judgment. How could I know then what I discovered later in life—that he is gentle, wise and loving?

For years I was needlessly bound in a straightjacket of fearful self-consciousness, always doing the most conservative thing so as not to attract negative attention, and sort of holding my breath until I could die and make it to heaven.

But God had other ideas. The experiences in the Salvation Army gave me the courage to love. Its motto is to "love the unlovable." Learning to love the unlovable enabled me to love myself as well. Isn't it ironic that God would choose such a shy, tense, and avoidant child like me to be a military officer, clinical psychologist, professional writer, university lecturer, and convention speaker? This year alone I have had my eighth major book published, and addressed convention crowds numbering in the thousands. I gave the opening speech at the American Association of Pastoral Counselors, in San Diego, and a paper at the American Psychological Association this past year.

Was I afraid? Yes. Did I have self-doubts? Yes. Did I feel God's presence? Yes. How did I feel afterward? Peaceful! One of the greatest lessons I have learned in life is a willingness to endure its hardships, which includes the negative experiences we all have along our journey. With Jesus' help, and the inward support of the Holy Spirit, we can learn to say yes! to life, even though we experience degrees of fear, doubt, and shyness along the way.

The key to growth is insight, new choices, persistence, the "courage of imperfection," prayer, and belief in God's grace.

Realize first of all that the Helpless Perspective is just a way of seeing things. If you remove your glasses of that color, you will see the world differently. Meanwhile, the world does not particularly care. It will go right on being the way it is. It is up to you and you alone to change the way you see things. The Holy Spirit will assist you greatly, if you desire. But do not expect him to do all the work. More than likely, he will create opportunities for you to respond in new and different ways, but the choice is always up to you.

There is a story told of a man in a flood who found himself stranded on a church steeple. He prayed vigorously for God to rescue him. A boat came by and the captain yelled at him to jump in, but he was too afraid. A raft came floating by. He could have jumped on, but it seemed just a bit too far. Finally, a helicopter hovered overhead and dropped down a ladder, but he was afraid to fly and rejected the opportunity.

The church then collapsed and the man drowned. He awakened in heaven, and immediately complained that he had prayed fervently to be rescued, but to no avail. Then he heard the voice of God say, "Who do you think sent the boat, the raft, and the helicopter?"

If you are an Avoidant personality, the first thing to do is to become aware of it without feeling crushed or persecuted. The second thing is to mobilize great energy to make a creative change. Get out of the destructive habit, most likely picked up in adolescent years, of seeing yourself as "stupid," "ugly," "a failure," "lazy," "selfish," "withdrawn," or "clumsy." Throw these negatives into the wastebasket as you would an outgrown pair of shoes.

No longer tolerate people, jobs, and situations that make you feel inadequate. Individuals functioning out of the Helpless Perspective have an uncanny knack for getting themselves involved with cruel and sadistic people and jobs, and then staying there forever because they do not feel that they have the right to leave or make a change. "What would they think of me?" But the bottom line is that they do not care about you. If they did, they would treat you with respect and courtesy.

Give yourself time to relax, to pray, to listen to yourself, to enjoy hobbies and activities you can do alone. In this way you can get in better touch with yourself.

Actively imagine yourself being more assertive. Model yourself after people you admire, and then exercise and strengthen those assertive skills in you.

Stop being so overprotective about your ego; it is tougher than you think. It bruises but never breaks. Better it should occasionally get hurt than that you should sit out the game of life on the bench. Your life is an adventure. Create what happens next.

Develop long-range goals in life, with highly specific short-range subgoals. Contemplate realistic ways to achieve these subgoals. Be the first to praise yourself for even the tiniest successes. Know that God praises your efforts too.

Tell yourself every night and every day that you are a unique individual who, as a participating actor in life's drama, can make things happen. You can change the direction of your entire life any time you choose to do so. With confidence in yourself, obstacles become challenges, and challenges turn into achievements. Shyness and avoidant tendencies then recede, for emotionally you are outgrowing the Helpless Perspective. You feel proud of the changes you make, and you ask God to continue assisting you in your birth as a confident and competent person.

You begin to forget about shyness. It is a bad habit, accidentally picked up in adolescence, that has no room in your maturing life. You dwell more and more on actualizing the talents, gifts, and special missions that God has planted deep within. You enjoy the pleasure of feeling these goals being accomplished, and these tasks being mastered.

Meditate on and plumb the depths of meaning of the following scriptures (all cited from the King James Version):

Psalm 27:1: "The Lord is my light and my salvation; whom shall I fear? the Lord is the strength of my life; of whom shall I be afraid?"

John 14:27: "Peace I leave with you, my peace I give unto you: not as the world giveth, give I unto you. Let not your heart be troubled, neither let it be afraid."

Romans 8:28: "And we know that all things work

together for good to them that love God, to them who are the called according to his purpose."

Romans 8:38-39: "For I am persuaded, that neither death, nor life, nor angels, nor principalities, nor powers, nor things present, nor things to come, nor height, nor depth, nor any other creature, shall be able to separate us from the love of God, which is in Christ Jesus our Lord."

Philippians 4:19: "But my God shall supply all your need according to his riches in glory by Christ Jesus."

2 Timothy 1:7: "For God hath not given us the spirit of fear; but of power, and of love, and of a sound mind."

1 John 4:18: "There is no fear in love; but perfect love casteth out fear."

And **Jude 24-25:** "Now unto him that is able to keep you from falling, and to present you faultless before the presence of his glory with exceeding joy, to the only wise God our Saviour, be glory and majesty, dominion and power, both now and ever. Amen."

We suggest you record on a cassette this entire sequence of scriptures which specifically and effectively address your inner fears. Listen to the cassette twice a day for the next two weeks.

Then each day review our own suggestions for outgrowing the Helpless Perspective and becoming a whole, vital personality.

Expect opposition. Anyone who currently has some type of neurotic control over you will be offended by your new attitudes and growth. Either renegotiate that relationship, or, at least for the time being, drop that relationship from your life. In its place, seek relationships that honestly recognize your growth and potential (these will be with people who have learned to love themselves, and therefore do not need to control other people), and that support you each step of the way.

You must become self-preserving, but in a healthy way this time. Formerly, you tried to preserve yourself through avoidance of the world and others. Now, preserve yourself only from truly toxic influences, welcoming the rest of your human experience as a great and grand adventure.

When you are beyond the fear threshold, nothing and no one can ever hold you back again. And for that you can both praise God and pat yourself on the back. You deserve it.

EXERCISES

1. List all the fears that are in your life right now. Then rank them by listing the greatest fear as number 1, the second as number 2, and so on. Now take this list to God in prayer, and tell him how deeply a part of your humanity, how deeply a part of your feelings of vulnerability it is. Ask him to keep this list always in mind, as well as all the good and great things he has planned for you, and try to forget it yourself for at least one evening or one week or one month. Put God to the test of how he can creatively and realistically help you. And notice as different problems begin to be resolved. Catch God being good at supporting your life and making you stronger.

2. Determine whether or not you have at least one or two caring people in your life with whom you can really "tell it like it is." If you have a dozen, then you are probably spreading yourself too thin. If you have only one, then you are probably too isolated from the wisdom of several counselors. Commit yourself to building some kind of network of supportive people who believe in you, but who will also level with you. This can be much more difficult than it sounds, so pray for the Holy Spirit's guidance all along the way. This guidance may not come easily, but it will come.

3. The scariest thing you may ever have to do in functioning from the Helpless Perspective is to develop self-trust, self-reliance, and authentic self-direction. You are going to have to take risks. There is no getting around it. But this does not mean you must jump into the deep end of the pool right away. Become willing to take tiny risks. That will be plenty of openness from God's point of view to get leverage to change your life for the better, and to build and nurture self-confidence, courage, and success. Remember the widow's mite of Scripture, and how Christ valued her for giving little with much to lose more than he did those who gave much with little too lose.

4. Realize that as an individual stuck in the Helpless Perspective you are actually in an "ideal" position to receive the assistance of the Holy Spirit in every aspect of your need. This is true because, of all the different personality styles we discuss in this book, you most easily experience humility. Humility is a perfect launching pad for future successes, wisdom, and growth. Just do not get stuck there! Balance it with courage. (And do not be proud of being humble!) See yourself succeeding. Hug yourself inside whenever you make even the smallest gain. As time goes by, you will gain the wholeness you long for, and become a braver and more courageous person than you ever imagined possible.

9

THE STRIVING PERSPECTIVE (STRENGTH POLARITY)

Our greatest glory is not in never falling or failing, but in rising every time this happens. I call this the courage of imperfection.

—Everett Shostrom

Of the four primary partial perspectives that Christians can build into their personalities and life-styles, the pattern of Striving Perspective may well be the most subtle.

Doesn't everyone admire the Christian who is industrious, busy, and perpetually on the go? Isn't it a great virtue to be "on fire for the kingdom of God," to be ready in all times and places to give your testimony, and to have seemingly ceaseless energy for Christian ministry? Don't we praise the person who weathers every storm, overcomes every temptation, and always has the victory?

If you are not already a bit suspicious of such a personality style, you will be both suspicious and wisely discerning shortly.

The Christian with a Striving Perspective is stuck on the Strength polarity of personality. Somewhere along the line of personality development, this person received the message that work, personal achievement, and competitive performance (to outshine those around, even if seemingly humble about doing so) are the most important things in life. Such people live and strive under what we term "the curse of perfectionism"— everything has to be done just right, which means, of course, according to their arbitrary standards. Anything less than perfect requires judgment, reprimand, and correction. This is why they are no fun to live, work, or even play with.

The striving business or church executive needs to have a perfectly efficient organizational machine in which people are treated like cogs in a wheel—they are manipulated as objects or statistics in order to achieve the Striving person's goals. The Striving housewife works herself to the bone, compulsively cleaning the house as though it were a museum showcase, not a home in which people enjoy getting together. The perfectionistic student is obsessed with mastering technique, memorizing trivia, and making high grades, all apart from any intrinsic interest or intrigue with the subject matter. The striving church worker becomes so preoccupied with "saving souls" or filling pews that he or she neglects completely the deeper opportunities for understanding, loving, and growing in relationships with others. Unfortunately, self-awareness and sensitivity to others all too often take a backseat to the compulsive need to achieve perfection. With the Striving Perspective alone running your life, you cannot help remaining always a spiritual infant.

Two examples from Scripture underscore the point. During the Last Supper with Christ, the disciples got into a big power struggle over who had striven the most: "And there was also a strife among them, which of them should be accounted the greatest" (Luke 22:24 *kjv*). We can now, looking back, realize how each one of them had a unique place in the fulfillment of God's plans, but for each of them at that moment an inner insecurity gave way to attempts to convince Jesus of their greatness, works, or sincerity so that they could receive the more important recognition. The moral of this particular encounter was that Jesus was not the least bit interested in their justifications of their own respective greatness. He ignored their words, and instead focused on the one major thing that had been the most important all along—their continued openness to him: "Ye are they which have continued with me in my temptations" (v. 28).

A second example is found in Luke 9:46-50 (*kjv*) where the disciples are again found reasoning among themselves who would become the greatest. And John, perhaps striving to demonstrate to all that he should be greatest, said to Jesus, "Master, we saw one casting out devils in thy name; and we forbad him, because he followeth not with us." Jesus debunked this attempt at self-glorification by stating, "Forbid him not: for he that is not against us is for us."

There is another important dimension to the stuckness and immaturity of the Striving Perspective: the idea that always acting strong is a virtue, and that experiencing your weaknesses, limitations, or needs for growth is to be avoided at all costs. Without the courage to disclose our secret fears, inferiority feelings, sins, faults, doubts, and hurts we cannot make progress toward becoming a whole person.

Jesus made no effort to conceal his own occasional feelings of weakness and vulnerability. In that most memorable event leading to the resurrection of Jesus' dear friend Lazarus, we find two equally memorable words—"Jesus wept" (John 11:35 *kjv*). The particular Greek word chosen by the biblical writer means "cried with real tears." This differentiated the sincere sadness welling up within Jesus' heart from the traditional type of ritualistic moaning, wailing, and chanting that funeral attendants were hired to do.

An even more poignant moment occurred in the Garden of Gethsemane when Jesus singled out Peter, James, and John—the closest of all his disciples—and asked them to be with him in his hour of greatest pain and vulnerability. Profoundly aware of his weakness, he said to them, "My soul is exceeding sorrowful unto death . . . and he went forward a little, and fell on the ground, and prayed that, if it were possible, the hour might pass from him" (Mark 13:34-35 KJV).

Somehow from the example of Jesus we too can find the courage to be fully human, to enjoy our strengths and competencies, to savor our achievements, while at the same time being aware of and admitting our weaknesses and needs.

But the individual stuck with the Striving Perspective forgets this principle, and instead focuses only on winning, looking good, being admired, acquiring power, and always being in control.

Author's personal comment—Ev:

I can identify with the Striving Perspective. Throughout my childhood my mother referred to me as "Momma's little soldier." She and my father had certain difficulties in their relationship, and somehow she unconsciously put the burden of responsible behavior onto me. So I never really had a childhood where I could romp and laugh and play.

Several years ago I spent a weekend in a self-discovery group. Each person had a chance to express to the group his or her goal in life that had been most important. I thought of a symbol that expressed my goal, an eagle on top of a mountain peak. It seems that most of my life I have tried to get to the top of the mountain, but now I find that it can be a very lonely place to be.

After we had shared our life goal with the group, we had a chance to role-play an opposite kind of experience. For me, it was becoming a little boy again and putting my head in the lap of a woman who role-played a kind and loving mother. I was moved to tears. I realized I had not received such love as a youngster, and that the attention I had received was mostly for doing things well and performing or earning my way.

So I have spent many of my adult years doing just that. But, thank God, this long awaited awareness has brought with it more relaxation and enjoyment of life. I no longer must weary myself trying to make things happen, or subconsciously compete with others for some kind of status or recognition. I am slowly learning how to love myself whether I achieve or not. And this new freedom brings me peace.

The person straightjacketed in the Striving Perspective is afraid of being judged inadequate or unworthy if perfectionistic standards are not met. The corollary is the assumption that play, fun, recreation, and the joy of intimate relationships with others are a waste of time. Hard, continuous work replaces love as the central goal of life. Achievement is the one note that the individual with a Striving Perspective plays compulsively day after day.

There is a saying that "God helps those who help themselves." Even though the saying has a degree of wisdom in it, it can easily become only a rationalization for putting more emphasis on performing, accomplishing, and getting ahead, than on loving oneself and others. The saying appears nowhere in the Bible.

The person with the Striving Perspective attempts to appear strong, competent, and capable at all times, and becomes a workaholic (see figure 7). As if this were not enough, the person dictates to others that they too should put their noses to the grindstone. Because Striving people seldom if ever admit weaknesses, they become equally intolerant of anyone else's feelings or needs. Spouse, children, and colleagues especially sense their tenseness, irritability, and distance. But their feedback gets little result, since the Striving individual is cocksure of being right, and therefore feels neither guilt nor empathy as he

Fig. 7   THE STRIVING PERSPECTIVE

or she heads off to start another project, found another church, buy another piece of property, attend another convention, or read another newspaper.

Having lost sensitivity to the gentle promptings of the Holy Spirit, Striving personalities may set out to accomplish very worthy goals in life, but can also end up, while achieving these goals, causing great confusion in the lives of those around them. They suffer the dual maladies of tunnel vision and emotional isolation.

It may take a divorce, a near fatal car accident, a child gone far astray, or a heart attack before they grow conscious of the shallowness of this life-style. Such a catastrophe may well be a blessing in disguise—an entreaty from God to slow down, relax more, let spiritual and psychological roots grow deeper and more sturdy before getting back into the mainstream of life.

In other words, Striving people need to give up their pride and learn humility. They need to open up more deeply to both God and caring others in order to remain balanced and less frantic, and feel more at home with just being themselves; and without all the big to-do they formerly made over their achievements. Two books that testify to such breakthroughs in awareness are *A Taste of New Wine*, by Keith Miller, and *I Ain't Much, but I'm All I've Got*, by Jess Lair.

Carried to the extreme, persons caught in the grip of the Striving Perspective are categorized by the *DSM III* as Compulsive (perfectionistic) and Narcissistic (self-absorbed). Though they may be the last to admit it, such individuals are unconsciously mesmerized by their own strengths. Other characteristics are as follows:

1. They are perfectionistic to the point of interfering with their ability to grasp the bigger picture. They believe so firmly that their way is the "right way" that they insist on others submitting to their style of doing things.

2. They are formal in manner, and stiff in their bodies.

Conversations with them have a tense and serious quality. They are carefully dressed, pedantic, correct, and excessively moralistic. They have an unnatural, constrained way about them.

3. They are stingy. This is because they put an overemphasis on possessions, since they have difficulty separating themselves from the objects they own and the status they possess.

4. They derive inordinate pleasure from classifying, indexing, organizing, and objectifying both people and things.

5. They are extremely aware of their relative status, which can make them very nervous or very overbearing, depending upon whether they feel threatened or accepted in a given situation.

6. Their consuming need is to give a good impression and to be in control. Since a show of any genuine tenderness, weakness, need, fault, or compromise could weaken their image of being like the Rock of Gibraltar, they abhor and avoid these tendencies.

7. They avoid themselves by seeking out new audiences for whom they can perform, or by creating new projects that have to be attended to.

8. They have spent little time developing their emotional, psychological, or spiritual selves. They may sense a nameless void within, but are so unaware of and phobic about such a reality that it only spurs them on to intensify projects and programs.

9. They are not "in-touch" people, and this is why they often reduce life's problems and difficulties to the fault of someone else.

Most probably the person stuck in the Striving Perspective was hurt early in life when he or she, like all children, felt psychological and spiritual hunger for positive affection and love from others. At a subconscious level, this person felt betrayed because the deep and vulnerable need was not met. No one needs to be at fault here. Parents generally do the best they know how, and often they know very little about healthy parenting. In addition, manipulative or neurotic parenting styles are passed down from generation to generation until someone takes a stand to unravel the neurosis and establish a healthier and more spiritually sound method of relating to one another within the family system.

We all fall victim to a certain degree of dis-ease and neurotic force in the formation of our personalities and in the working out of our relationships with parents, siblings, friends, spouse, our own children, and with God. Such is the human dilemma. And such is the universal human need for salvation to heal our souls and psychological insight to heal our emotional wounds.

You may now see clearly how our theory of personality and of family and interpersonal relationships interfaces with the personal need for insight, healing, and growth.

Author's personal comment—Dan:
It was during teenage years, while gazing upward toward the brilliantly sparkling New Mexico night skies, that I experienced a kind of astro-hunger—a passion to know just where and how I fit in amidst those myriad stars. But my entrapment, in those days, to a Striving Perspective, made it seem difficult ever to feel close to God or people.

That gap is gone now—or at least it is not nearly so wide as it used to be. It's taken innumerable people loving me, and giving me space to be, as well as what seem like thousands of risks on my part to put aside my façade and come out with my own vulnerable feelings, to make this happen.

I still grow anxious sometimes if I begin to feel that I'm not as competent as I "should" be, or as close to God as I "ought" to be, or as good a human being and Christian as

I "must be." But those times seem less and less common.

What I'm most happy about is that by applying to my own life the LAWS of personality we are teaching, I have made satisfying gains in my own quest to be myself, to be open to God, and to discover my mission one day at a time. I'm not sure another person can truly imagine all the self-doubt, guilt, anxiety, depression, frustration, confusion, and at times loneliness, that has gone into the making of who I now am.

The positive aspect of my addiction to the Striving Perspective and the Compulsive life-style was that I had to do my homework in life. It wasn't as much a choice to get my Ph.D by twenty-seven as it was a compulsion. But once the work was done it became time to slow down and to start learning more from life itself than from thousands of solitary hours in the library.

I can see now how being stuck on the Strength polarity would have made me a snob, a know-it-all, and a bore (all of which I have certainly been). But now all that seems far less important than the importance of my adventure with God and people wherever that adventure may lead.

This July, I was in New Mexico once again to celebrate a twenty-year high school reunion. We were together three days and nights, and what struck me most of all was that no one knew or cared that I had become a clinical psychologist. Out in California I've been called "Dr." or at least "Dan" for close to twelve years. But back in New Mexico when we classmates met and hugged each other, roles and titles had no meaning. I was "Danny," the prankster and attention-getter (another side to my personality) of two decades ago. I'll probably never outgrow that part of me, but the compulsive, overly serious Striving Perspective was no longer there.

I welcomed the hugs and returned them exuberantly.

And on the last night I took a drive to Storrie Lake, got out of the car, pulled up my jacket collar against the cool breeze, and looked skyward. "Thank you. I know you love me now—just as I am—thank you," I whispered.

People with a rigid Striving Perspective are always trying to earn love, admiration, and approval. But even when these come they find themselves too busy to really enjoy them. Busyness is a way of life. But they must realize that God's love is an act of grace, and does not depend on how much one accomplishes. In the frenzied compulsion for constant activity that can typify their lives as Strivers, there is no time left to experience this grace. There is only a blinding blur of busyness in the effort to maintain the illusion of always being strong and having everything under control.

Christian culture sometimes encourages the Striving Perspective by offering praise and plaques for the most service projects undertaken, the most souls led to Christ, the most attendance at all church functions, or the most hours spent in prayer. These projects are never wrong in themselves. They become misguided only when compulsive and subconsciously competitive attitudes are present.

We need to realize how far such a life-style departs from the truly biblical principle of resting and trusting in the Lord for every facet of our daily and yearly living. Without that principle, we become so obsessed with doing good works or carrying on worthwhile projects that we leave the Holy Spirit on the sidelines and function without his anointing or guidance.

To enable the influx of the balancing polarity of Weakness, which is the source of the virtue of humility, to become more present in your personality, we suggest you record the following scriptures (all cited from the King James Version) on a cassette and play the recording back to yourself twice a day for a period of two weeks. While doing so, ask the Holy Spirit to reveal any tendency you may have toward the Striving Perspective, and actively seek his guidance to balance doing with being, and Strength with Weakness:

Zechariah 4:6: "Not by might, nor by power, but by my spirit, saith the Lord of hosts."

2 Corinthians 12:8-10: "For this thing I besought the Lord thrice, that it might depart from me. And he said unto me, My grace is sufficient for thee: for my strength is made perfect in weakness. Most gladly therefore will I rather glory in my infirmities, that the power of Christ may rest upon me. Therefore I take pleasure in infirmities, in reproaches, in necessities, in persecutions, in distresses for Christ's sake: *for when I am weak, then am I strong*" (italics ours).

Psalm 103:13, 14: "Like as a father pitieth his children, so the Lord pitieth them that fear him. For he knoweth our frame; he remembereth that we are dust."

Isaiah 40:29, 31: "He giveth power to the faint; and to them that have no might he increaseth strength . . . they that wait upon the Lord shall renew their strength; they shall mount up with wings as eagles."

James 4:6: "God resisteth the proud, but giveth grace unto the humble."

1 Peter 5:6: "Humble yourselves therefore under the mighty hand of God, that he may exalt you in due time."

James 1:5: "If any of you lack wisdom, let him ask of God, that giveth to all men liberally, and upbraideth not; and it shall be given him."

Psalm 37:4-5: "Delight thyself also in the Lord; and he shall give thee the desires of thine heart. Commit thy way unto the Lord; trust also in him; and he shall bring it to pass."

Psalm 51:17: "The sacrifices of God are a broken spirit: a broken and a contrite heart, O God, thou wilt not despise."

Isaiah 57:15: "For thus saith the high and lofty One that inhabiteth eternity, whose name is Holy; I dwell in the high and holy place, with him also that is of a contrite and humble spirit, to revive the spirit of the humble, and to revive the heart of the contrite ones."

What the person who is outgrowing the partial personality of the Striving Perspective needs to realize is that everytime he or she feels perplexed or overwhelmed by life, the feeling of weakness and vulnerability can be a royal occasion to draw near to God or to a trusted spouse or friend. In disclosing our weaknesses, we give others the opportunity to give to us. They may not have all the answers, but they can bring needed comfort, support, and encouragement. "No man is an island," said John Donne, and the mature sharing of our deepest anxieties, self-doubts, or fears enables us to release these feelings quickly and receive empathy and affirmation in their place.

If we desire to encounter and learn to trust the Holy Spirit in our lives, we must become honestly aware of our many needs. Apart from God's plans and resources, our lives become partial and fragmented. The more we assert willful control, the more fragmented we become, because the truth is that we do profoundly need a strong connection to God and to significant others to find meaning and inner contentment in life. This is why the Bible, from Genesis though Revelation, emphasizes that God meets face to face with those who admit their need, while resisting people who are rigid and striving in their self-assured sense of independence.

God is far more accepting of our real weaknesses than most of us realize. He welcomes our need as an opportunity to draw near to us in a way that is tangible and that really makes a difference in how things turn out. If you do not believe that this is true, then we challenge you to ask God today or tonight to assist you in solving one of your most difficult and draining problems. Admit that you are stymied, and tell him you will give him full credit if he helps you out of this one!

That can be the beginning of a move from the Striving

Perspective to a Spirit-filled personality. But the follow through is just as important as the beginning. Keep asking God to guide and assist you, and to inspire and direct you. You will be amazed at the absolutely personal and confidential way he responds to your honest and open prayers. The God of the Bible is neither an abstract idea nor a convenient fiction. He is an ever present personal presence who has a passionate love for you—just as you are, right now.

EXERCISES

1. If you are functioning from the Striving Perspective, then first thank God that you have already learned such valuable lessons as discipline, concentration, dedication, frustration tolerance, and goal-setting. But once these lessons in life-style have been learned, it becomes vital to balance them with others.

2. When you live from the Striving Perspective, there is too much of you, and too little of God at work in your personality. Build a desire to reach beyond the ivory tower of self-assurance or independence. Love is the doorway through which we pass from solitude to kinship with humanity. Our passage through the doorway of love may include all of the fear or travail of our original passage through the birth canal into this world. And the result may be just as revolutionary: we are delivered into a whole new experience and understanding of life. Try this week to listen for your child's request for help with homework; to give special time to your spouse, time uncluttered by a flurry of worries or projects; to use your sense of self-confidence to encourage someone who is discouraged; to spend time listening in a conversation instead of always

talking or controlling; to realize your insignificance in the universe compared to the life of a redwood tree, the depth of the ocean, or the vastness of the Milky Way.

3. Face inwardly your hidden sense of inferiority, which you may be surprised and defensive to learn of. Accept that portion of yourself that wants to get to the top of the pyramid by tromping over everyone else's shoulders. You must learn to love and raise that insecure child inside your psyche, so that you can be truly mature. Try to find someone to talk with openly about these things.

4. List on a piece of paper the advantages you gain from being a tireless worker who can only rest when the job is done, and done right: for instance habits of discipline, perseverance, and stick-to-it-ive-ness. Thank God for them. Beethoven would never have written his symphonies without being totally absorbed in his work. But in interpersonal relations he failed miserably. That is your Achilles' heel too.

   Now make a new list and fill it in with behavior you need to learn—playing, laughing, doing nothing, taking occasional naps. Notice that you start feeling uneasy and guilty making this second list. But instead of stopping this project in self-discovery, utilize your compulsiveness to finish it. List the ways your preoccupation with work takes you away from precious and needed time with spouse, children, friends, and new life adventures. Decide that, with help from the Holy Spirit, you are going to become more receptive to "spontaneous people time."

5. If the Compulsive neurosis really has you by the throat, then you need to pray earnestly to be freed from it. It will never go away on its own. It controls you. Pray that you will control it in the future—starting now.

   Become creative about how you can make compulsive tendencies work for you. As a compulsive reader, explore how you might develop writing or teaching skills, whether at the lay or professional levels, so as to pass on what you learn. As a compulsive housekeeper, start searching for new ways to connect with adults, such as taking community college courses, finishing a degree, joining a self-discovery group, or in some other way encountering people and culture.

6. Learn to relax and enjoy the things around you that you might otherwise be too preoccupied to even notice. The beauty of a flower, the striking configuration of clouds in the sky, the smells of the ocean or of good food or of mown grass, the smile of a child, the embrace of a loved one, the serenity acquired from prayer.

7. Ask for more perceptual feedback from friends or loved ones. How do they really see you? Back off from your old defensive stance that would discount or counter everything they say. Instead develop a capacity to be surprised, curious, and even intrigued by what they say.

    You will be amazed at how honest and objective people can be when you really ask them to be—when you are not trying to make them say certain things, but just allowing and respecting their emotional and perceptual feedback.

10

BEYOND MANIPULATION

To trust God is to be enabled to trust oneself at the very core of one's being . . . Once we have been grasped by God's affirmation of us, we have experienced love at the very heart of things. And the power of that love begins to make all things in this fragmented world whole again.

—Theodore Runyon

You can now understand how and why a person's God-given actualizing tendencies can be thwarted—how authentic responses to life through Love, Assertiveness, Weakness, and Strength can be blocked by the hindrance of a partial personality perspective. What God intended to be a rhythmic and flowing swing into each of these dimensions as each new situation might require becomes a rigid adherence to just one or two polarities as a defensive way of relating to self and others.

To function out of sync with your whole personality potential is to live in a self-defeating way. We define self-defeating behavior as manipulative behavior and creative behavior as actualizing behavior. As shown in figure 8, actualizing behavior is simply manipulative behavior expressed more creatively. It gives us all hope that psychological and spiritual maturity is within our potential when we realize that our manipulative patterns of stuckness need only be modified and transformed for our lives to become more whole and healthy.

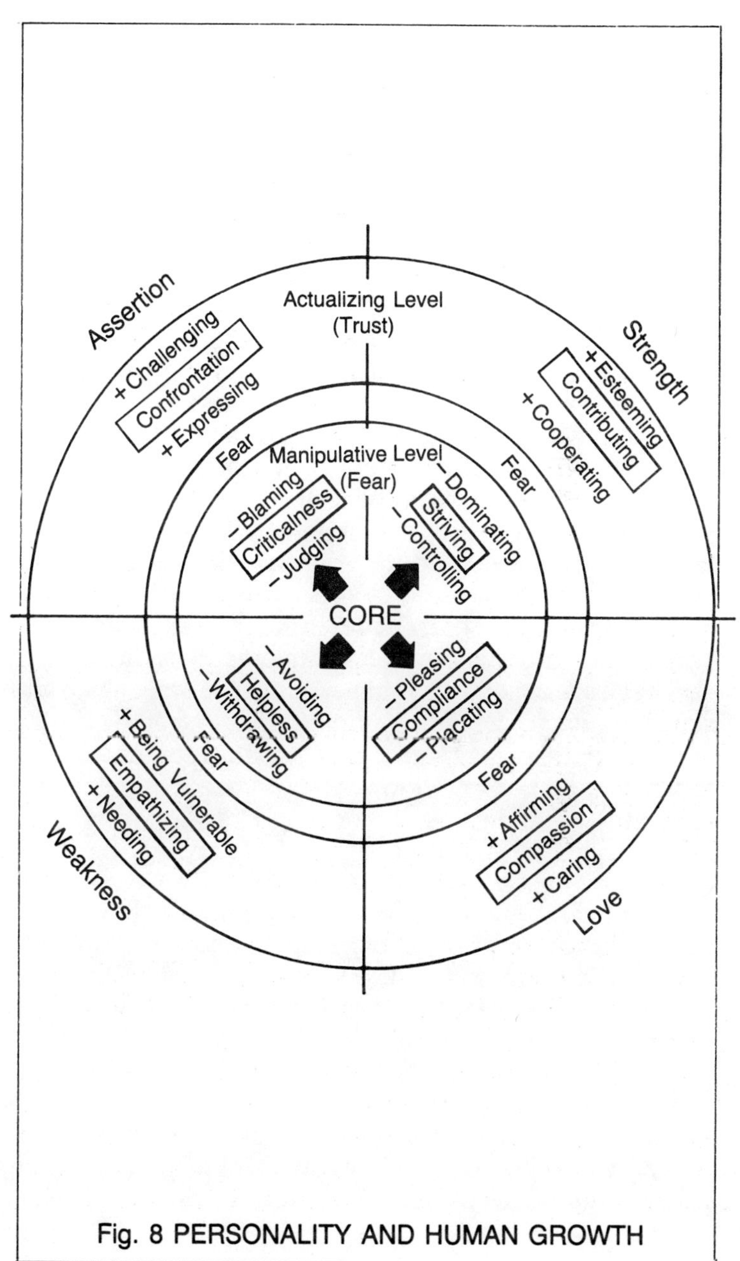

Fig. 8 PERSONALITY AND HUMAN GROWTH

In figure 8 the innermost ring of descriptions represents major manipulative tactics of each polarity. Far too many of us unknowingly live out our lives with these partial and self-defeating behaviors. It makes sense to view these behaviors as being defensive, learned patterns, based on the "Ring of Fear" that encompasses the core. The eight manipulative behaviors within this band of fear reflect constriction of the personality and a stifling of the Compass Points of the Self into the partial perspectives of Critical, Compliant, Helpless, and Striving behavior. Manipulative behavior involves four fundamental characteristics: deception, unawareness, control, and cynicism—and it can be unlearned! The descriptive words shown between the inner circle of manipulative tactics and the dotted outermost boundaries of the personality are propeople and progrowth behaviors that enhance self and others whenever used sincerely.

Keep in mind that our theory encompasses the positive and negative aspects of living at the same time. Once you see how you are stuck in an ultimately self-defeating behavior pattern, you can see at the same moment exactly in which direction and how much you need to stretch into specific new behaviors in order to regain a sense of core-centeredness and personality health.

By studying figure 8, you can also become aware of how someone troublesome to you has been manipulating you, and, once aware, you can discover exactly what new behavior to adopt to break that person's unhealthy hold and initiate the possibility of a more mutually rewarding relationship.

Let's say that a friend of yours always leaves you feeling somehow nervous and uncomfortable, and you have never discovered why. By looking at the diagram, you realize that she functions mainly from the Assertion polarity, using blaming and attacking as her primary behaviors. No wonder you have felt bad about yourself after spending any time at all with her. All she does is complain and gripe about the world, and point out your shortcomings. What has thrown you off for so long is that she seems so confident about what she says—as if she knows it all, and you have a lot to learn.

Now you realize that she spends her energies criticizing everything and everybody just to distract you from discovering what a superficial person she is. Subconsciously, she reasons that if minute attention is paid to everyone else's flaws (yours included), no one will point out her own. She is right. But it is self-defeating in the end, because she tactically avoids all constructive criticism from others (which could do her a world of good, but which would certainly be ego-deflating at first), and she also severely limits what she or anyone else can derive from the relationship, since for all practical purposes the relationship becomes simply an extension of her boring, stagnant personality. Her hidden ring of inner fear (about which she may be totally unaware) blocks all growth and puts an impenetrable barrier between her and other people, as well as distorting her perception of God.

By understanding objectively that your friend is stuck on the Assertion polarity with manipulative patterns of blaming and attacking, you can: (1) tell her that you would like her to work at being more positive and not just trying to get your attention in negative ways, (2) quit trying to win her approval by pleasing and placating her by your passive listening, (3) work on building and keeping a positive sense of self-esteem in her presence (this stretches you out on your own Strength polarity), (4) confront her each time she attempts to undercut and criticize you or someone else (this will stretch you out on your Assertion polarity), or (5) continue to humor her by listening, but work on not being affected by anything she says (which involves faith in your own objective analysis of her criticisms rather than a subjective, emotional response). Any and all of these creative responses are better than remaining naive toward the manipulative nature of her communications and continuing to be hooked by her negativity.

The marvelous aspect about being human—created in God's image—is that we do have free will to choose our own attitudes and responses and to break rigid behavioral chains, whether those rigid patterns originate from within ourselves or from someone with whom we associate. We are not like grasshoppers, birds, or ants. We can choose.

In sharp contrast to manipulative behavior, actualizing behavior is characterized by honesty, awareness, freedom, and trust (see table). The change from manipulation to actualization comprises a continuum, and involves a transition *from* deadness and deliberateness *to* aliveness and spontaneity. The left-hand column of the table depicts characteristics of behavior located in the ring of fear, or manipulative level, of figure 8. The right-hand column describes more positive attitudes and behaviors located in the actualizing level of figure 8.

Utilizing figure 8, we can look at each of the polarities and show how each manipulative tendency can be transformed into a positive, actualizing counterpart.

From the Assertion polarity arise asserting and expressing, the actualizing counterparts of blaming and attacking. The person who expresses assertion or even anger in diplomatic and aboveboard ways exhibits the virtue of *confrontation with caring,* or "speaking the truth in love." Jesus often expressed this trait when he felt frustrated by someone's stubbornness, deceitfulness, or competitiveness. On numerous occasions he confronted both his closest disciples as well as his deadliest enemies. What he did not do was to use spitefulness, vindictiveness, or hatred. He expressed his irritation quickly and honestly, and then moved on, often to feelings of concern and compassion.

TABLE

FUNDAMENTAL CHARACTERISTICS OF MANIPULATIVE VS. ACTUALIZING BEHAVIOR

Manipulation	Actualization
1. *Deception* (Phoniness):	1. *Honesty* (Transparency, Genuineness, Authenticity):
The use of tricks, techniques, and maneuvers. Putting on an act, role-playing to create an impression. "Putting on" feelings to fit the occasion.	The ability to honestly be one's feelings, whatever they might be. The use of candidness to express genuinely the self.
2. *Unawareness* (Deadness, Boredom):	2. *Awareness* (Responsivity, Aliveness, Interest:
Having tunnel vision. Hearing and seeing only what one wishes. Captive to own rigid biases.	Looking fully and listening to self and others. Open to new information and discovery.
3. *Control* (Closed, Deliberate):	3. *Freedom* (Spontaneity, Openness):
Playing life like a chess game. Appearing relaxed, yet very controlled, concealing motives from "opponents." Needing things to be always the same. Fighting change.	An adventurer in life. Allowing for novelty, change, growth, and surprise. Having freedom to be core self and to express all polarities of personality.
4. *Cynicism* (Distrust):	4. *Trust* (Faith):
Being basically distrustful of self and others. Deep down, distrust of human nature or divine impulse. Seeing only two options to all relations—to control or be controlled.	Having deep trust of self and openness to inspirations that come from deep within. Trusting God to be Companion and Helper along life's way. Preferring mutuality to control.

127

On the Love polarity, the manipulative patterns of pleasing and placating are transformed into the actualizing traits of affirming and caring. There is freedom to praise, nurture, and support both oneself and others, without burdening others with expectations of having to return the favor. Built into the combination of affirming and caring are firmness and warmth. From these qualities emerges the virtue of *compassion,* a sure mark of the actualizing Christian.

On the Weakness polarity, withdrawing and avoiding need to be transformed into feeling vulnerable and empathizing. These actualizing traits, in turn, are cornerstones of the virtue of *empathy.* To be empathetic means to be "touched" by the needs or distress of another. The Good Samaritan showed this virtue. But it finds its most perfect human expression in Christ, the God-man. The author of Hebrews makes a passionate point (5:8 KJV) that although Jesus was filled, anointed, and blessed without measure by the Holy Spirit, he still experienced fully the painful negatives of human life: "Though he were a Son, yet learned he obedience by the things which *he suffered*" (italics ours). And Paul makes this point to underscore the unique mediation between God and every person, which Jesus makes possible. He is a High Priest who has perfect empathy for every individual human being, because he knows from his own direct experience how painful, cruel, and harsh life can sometimes be. "Seeing then that we have a great high priest, that is passed into the heavens, Jesus the Son of God, let us hold fast our profession. For we have not an high priest which cannot be touched with the feeling of our infirmities; but was in all points tempted like as we are, yet without sin. Let us therefore come boldly unto the throne of grace, that we may obtain mercy, and *find grace* to help in time of need" (Hebrews 4:14-15 KJV, italics ours).

In other words, Jesus' own personal experiences with human weakness, with uncertainty, vulnerability, hurt, and helplessness, make him the most empathetic Friend and Counselor you could ever hope to meet. It is for this reason that we view Jesus not only as the greatest preacher, but also the wisest psychologist who ever lived.

In regard to the last polarity, the Strength polarity, the egocentric manipulating behaviors, competing and controlling, need to be transformed into the interpersonal qualities, cooperating and contributing. To repeat, John Donne said, "No man is an island." And none of us can develop fully by being a dictator or controller of others. The person stuck on the Strength polarity needs to develop more trust in others, so that genuine self-esteem and esteem of others can occur. To again expand our psychological knowledge by looking at Christ, he could have been the most clever dictator who ever lived. But in the most unusual and actualizing turn of events, he, the One who was greatest of all, became the servant of all. He delegated regal power to fishermen and tax collectors, and trusted harlots and thieves with his friendship. He used his strength to inspire, support, and enable others to realize their own full potential—and the Spirit of Christ continues to do this same thing in our hearts and lives today. The virtue that arises from Strength, rightly utilized, is *self esteem* and esteem of others.

As you can see, real wisdom is built into the warp and woof of human nature. Once we have opened our deepest selves to Christ, then our human natures become not our enemy but rather the very channel through which the divine Spirit moves to vitalize our personalities. It is as though God intended a sensitive set of checks and balances in order to create a reliable source of guidance and inspiration within each person. And at the same time he created a vacuum in the deepest core—a place that only he can fill and fulfill.

It is our belief that as you come to live from your core in actualizing ways more and more each day, you will experience a connectedness to others and to God that will fill your life with genuinely positive happenings. There will be inner peace. There will be excitement and aliveness. There will be adventure. And, yes, there will also be occasional adversity, confusion, and pain. But the positive inertia created by the artesian well of inspiration will always bring fresh meaning and renewal after the hard times. As the Psalmist said, "weeping may endure for a night, but joy cometh in the morning" (Psalm 30:5 KJV).

We all engage in partial perspectives and manipulative behavior at least some of the time, and every one of us exaggerates one or more of the personality polarities. To do so is only human, and need not be considered "sick" or "sinful" as much as unfortunate and unnecessary.

Most of us stick to one polarity because somewhere in our development we found that it worked for us, it helped us to get what we wanted. We have become comfortable with it and extremely uncomfortable with some or all of the others. If, for example, as a child, you had a father who melted when you treated him lovingly, who gave you what you wanted when you fawned over him adoringly, you may have hit upon the notion that the way to succeed in life is by being lovable. You placed an exaggerated value on love. If you were surrounded by people who cowered and gave in when you got angry, you may have decided that assertion gets you what you want, and thus you put an exaggerated value on aggressiveness.

Every polarity that you are capable of feeling and expressing, can serve you. But if you come to rely on one to the exclusion of others, if you begin to call upon that polarity (love, assertion, weakness, or strength) in every situation, you have formed a pattern of manipulation and a distorted perception of life that "justifies" that manipulation. It is a pattern that can—and already may have—severely damaged your relationships with yourself and others. Yet in spite of the harm these patterns cause, you stick with them. They are comfortable and safe. They are easy to rationalize by claiming, "Well, that's just the way I am." We rigorously challenge that claim. You, as a manipulator, may act that way, but it is not the way you really are. It is not who you are. We believe that who you are, deep in your core, is a fully expressive, totally alive human being—an actualizer, not a slave to your manipulations.

But the excitement of being totally alive can be short-circuited by one-sided development. If, let's say, you relied consistently upon your strength, you would almost become your strength. You would constantly be showing the world a mask of strength, while denying your weakness. In so doing, you would render yourself incapable of using your weakness in situations that demand it, like saying you are sorry or admitting it when you do not know the answers or are in a situation over your head. You become like a four-cylinder engine constantly trying to run on only one cylinder. Like that engine, you can chug along, but only with great effort and at the expense of smooth, effortless operation.

John Stevens, in *Gestalt Is,* suggests that a big part of manipulation is intention—the mental effort of trying or striving. As soon as we get intention involved, he says, our focus shifts from the spontaneity of the present to the goal-orientation of the future. Instead of expressing ourselves right now, we manipulate people according to the way we expect them to be in the future. Instead of relating to people—that is, being with them as Christ so easily was, we are manipulating or doing to them. Every manipulation is in its own way an attempt to impress and control others. In contrast, actualizing expression is a genuine "letting go" and "letting be" experience.

Any act can be an expression of relating or manipulating. We can smile out of joy in seeing you, or we can smile to make it look that way. We can cry as a result of genuine sorrow for you, or we can cry to make you feel guilty.

Expression is a welling up, an unrehearsed outpouring; it needs no response. Manipulation is calculated and demands a response. Stevens says, "Expression is a fountain; manipulation is a whirlpool. With expression I feel moved; with manipulation I feel sucked in, drained . . . with manipulation life becomes a wrestling match, with expression, it's more like a dance."

Relating without manipulation is the experience of expressing yourself effortlessly. It is based on the assumption that if we become aware of our core feelings in the heart, the truth of our being will express itself.

Because all of us are fearful of expressing our polarities, fear becomes a barrier. But that fear can be overcome by new, enlightened choice—deliberately, as we become emotionally growing and maturing adults. The perils of childhood hurts and misconceptions no longer have a grip on us. We break the stranglehold, move through our fears, and gain contact with a full range and intensity of feelings. Those feelings were there all along, to assist in our journey through life, and can help us once we are willing to let go of fear and the security of rigidity.

The first step involves admitting you are afraid to express the fear, because the very act of expressing it is frightening in itself. This usually causes the other person to invite you to express it anyway. Once you express the fear, the way is open for you to awaken and experience each and every polarity. You learn to exercise courage regularly in living and relating more spontaneously and experimentally. You even learn to value change—to look forward to it, and to enjoy it while it is happening.

In doing so you make contact with the real person in others and you discover over and over again that unique individual who is the real you.

EXERCISES

1. Take out a sheet of paper and draw a large circle in the middle. Now slice this "pie" into four pieces, which represent proportionately how much energy you spend each week investing in the following interpersonal activities: empathy, confrontation, compassion, esteem. Which slice is the smallest? Can you think of ways to make that slice of energy more equal to the rest in weeks to come? Which slice is the largest? Could it be that the largest slice represents an overreliance on one of the polarities, and consequently some kind of neglect of the rest? How would you like your interpersonal "energy pie" to look in the future?

2. Spend some time in thought and prayer about at least one relationship in which you are currently feeling somewhat confused and manipulated. Find where the other person fits into figure 8, and determine his or her ulterior motive in keeping a stagnant, no-win relationship with you in which he or she always ends up on top. How can you actively change your responses and reactions to this person? If you are willing to take the necessary risks, promise yourself that you will try new behaviors based on your new overview of the situation.

3. Do you really believe that Jesus personally experienced the weaknesses of human nature deeply enough to understand and empathize with everything in your weak side? Why or why not?

4. As an experiment in therapeutic prayer-imagery, can you for a moment bring into awareness the deepest, darkest secret from your past? Something you feel very

ashamed of or embarrassed about. Or something that you have never quite been able to believe that God could understand or forgive. Now with eyes shut visualize yourself talking face to face with Jesus about it. Confess it openly. Put fear aside. You are going to really test God with this one, so take all the stops out and lay it on the line. Picture Jesus' face, calm and steadied, as he hears your story. Now let him reach out and gently touch your shoulder—a touch that conveys support and acceptance. Look deep into his eyes and notice the twinkle. Perhaps he is proud of you for being so bold . . . for being so honestly in contact with your weakness. Is there the hint of a smile on his lips?

5. Write on a sheet of paper all the ways in which you now know you manipulate people. Then write in big, bold letters the word *fear* across the page. Now, if you are willing to give up the masks and go for deeper, more honest, self-expression, crumple the paper in your fist. Feel your power, your courage to face fear and move through it. Throw the paper in the wastebasket. Feel your determination to let go of the control you have tried to master, and just be yourself more and more with people. Feel the peacefulness that comes when the burden of manipulation is thrown off. Ask God to be with you in a very real way this week and this year—to heal your fears, inspire your creativity, and touch your core.

11

THE HEALING POWER OF LOVE

Fear hath torment . . . but perfect love casteth out fear.

—1 John 4:18

The one word that explains the bottom line motivation of people who retreat into partial personality patterns is fear. Since this is a difficult and sometimes brutal planet to be born on and live in, it is understandable how fear can come to dominate our inner cores, and block healthy growth and self-actualization.

Our central thesis, and our experience in thousands of therapeutic relationships, however, shows that "perfect love casts out fear" (1 John 4:18 RSV). When you feel understood and accepted, you relax and open up. You become less defensive and more interested in how to get better results in your life and relationships. A warm interpersonal climate, whether it be in a clinical psychologist's office, between spouses, or even between strangers, begins a process of truth-seeking, soul-searching, and healthy self-expression.

Author's personal comment—Dan:

Years ago I spent a year of Sundays visiting the county jail in Albuquerque, New Mexico, and talking to inmates about their lives, their choices, and the Lord.

One day I asked the guard about a door that stirred my curiosity. "Oh, that's the cell for total isolation. It's what these men fear most, and it's where we put the worst ones."

"Who's in there now?" I asked.

"Oh, he's a bad one. A real murderer. No conscience. Just goes berserk and kills people. Nobody goes near him."

I said, "Can I talk to him through the opening in the door?"

"OK," he said . . . "it's your life."

I spoke to the man and asked him how he ever got into such a predicament, how he ever lost so much of himself that he had to be shut away by others in such a dark hole.

He talked a little about a brutal childhood, and then he caught himself. "Hey, don't you realize I could reach through these bars and break your neck right now?"

"Yes, I do," I said. He was right, but I didn't back up. I said, "You know, you have a brain, you have a heart, you have intelligence, feelings, and aspirations. Why don't you do something about it? I believe that God will help you if you try."

Tears formed in his eyes, and then the guard pulled me away.

I don't know what happened to that man. Or what he chose to do with his life.

I do know that a warm interpersonal climate changes things. It makes us want to talk and disclose the deepest secrets of our souls. And we all need to open up now and then so that we can take inventory, and also so that we can be cleansed of pent-up, unfinished emotions that cloud our minds and block our trust in God and in our life mission.

Antigrowth forces that interrupt our personality development can range in intensity all the way from mild to devastating. We are all vulnerable. Vulnerability is our heritage from the planet on which we are born. Depending upon some combination of what happens to us and what inner resources we have to respond with, we all waver somewhere along the continuum, from full aliveness and vitality at one end to emotional and spiritual deadness at the other. Some of us learn to cope and others don't. Why that division exists is a mystery. But the mandate that Christ left to us is to "judge not" because none of us can encompass the total picture of how perfect love, mercy, and justice are being mixed together in both our neighbor's and our own lives.

The far more important truth is that we can learn to facilitate our own growth as well as to seek the psychological and spiritual well-being of those around us. This means taking responsibility to ensure we are both using and expanding the knowledge that we have. It also means that we learn to rely upon the Holy Spirit in a very real and tangible way.

God's loving us perfectly does not guarantee that we will always feel loved. The sun always shines on the earth, but sometimes a cloud, or nighttime even, temporarily blocks out the warmth that the earth receives. So it is with the growing Christian. Life has its peak experiences and its lows. There are times of oasis, and times of desert; times of utter confidence and times of self-alienation and doubt. There are times of ecstatic awareness of God's presence, and times when our prayers seem to bounce off the ceiling. But for the growing Christian—the actualizing Christian—even pain, confusion, frustration, and struggle are inspired tutors. In our hearts, we learn to say with Christ, "Not my will, but thine, be done" (Luke 22:42 KJV), and with Job, "Though he slay me, yet will I trust in him" (Job 13:15 KJV).

The actualizing life is based on more than just good times or good feelings. It is based on the courage to know the truth about oneself and one's destiny. This is why faith is at the heart of the Spirit-filled personality. The writer of Hebrews said, "But without faith it is impossible to please him: for he that cometh to God must believe that he is, and that he is a rewarder of them that diligently seek him" (11:6 *KJV*). Only faith can be open to God's sovereignty whatever the circumstances. Faith can penetrate the mystery of God's perfect love even when human understanding is darkened.

To change from superficial, defensive, and manipulative living to actualizing living does not require that we become something different from what we are. It simply means living more and more from our core, which comes to be infused in the most intimate way with God's creative Spirit (see again figure 8). Integrating the spiritual urges, promptings, and guidance from within with a continual willingness to express ourselves through the compass points of Love, Assertiveness, Weakness, and Strength, enables us to become more fully alive as life progresses. Middle and old age become opportunities for an increase in our personal powers and resources, even while the body itself gradually declines.

Senility is more often loss of the desire to grow and expand than it is an inevitable, physical impairment. Many teenagers become "senile" because, for whatever reasons, they lose the will to struggle for hope and meaning. In many ways, senility is often truly a personal choice.

Ashley Montagu writes in his book *Growing Young* that what characterizes *actualizing* human beings, whether infant, adolescent, or elderly, is "curiosity . . . imaginativeness; playfulness; open-mindedness; willingness to experiment; flexibility; humor; energy; receptiveness to new ideas; honesty; eagerness to learn; and perhaps the most pervasive and the most valuable of all, the need to love" (p. 2).

Some Christians believe that wholeness will happen automatically as soon as they come into a personal relationship with Jesus Christ. However, one of the mysteries of the Christian faith is that while we have the peace of Jesus' presence, we still have creative tension. This is because we are in the process of growing and becoming. To say it another way, Christianity affirms that the kingdom of God is at hand, yet at the same time it has not yet fully come. The Holy Spirit is in the world and in your personality as a Christian, yet at the same time you are still not a perfectly loving and wise being. To acknowledge this fact is to open yourself to God's continued molding and sculpturing of your personality, to avail yourself of his influence, an influence that gradually shapes you into what you ultimately can be.

The Holy Spirit is water in the clay of our lives. Although we may be initially skeptical or resistant, God is patiently willing to keep adding the influence of the Spirit to our lives until the personality is supple enough to be worked and molded.

In the twentieth century we are tempted to trust our lives to many influences other than the Holy Spirit: scientific sophistication, job and money, effects of drugs or newly spouted philosophies, acquisition of material goods, images of prestige from culture, or even rigid religious dogma.

But if we truly want to integrate culture, family, work, play and openness to God, it takes an exceptional courage —the courage to bear and benefit from the seemingly contradictory pulls and pressures of our day; the courage to trust the Holy Spirit to guide us toward authentic personal solutions to complex human dilemmas. This is the courage we invite the reader to exercise.

The Holy Spirit wants to form in and through our individual personalities and life circumstances a unique expression of Christlikeness. That expression takes into account every dimension of our lives—genetic and physical makeup, metabolic and hormonal systems, emotions, experiences in the environment, place in culture and history, special calling and destiny, and our profound and most special relationship with Jesus Christ in this life and in the life to come.

It is noteworthy that the Greek word used in the New Testament to characterize the activity of the Holy Spirit in the human personality is *dunamis*. This probably looks familiar because it is the root word from which our words *dynamo* and *dynamite* have evolved. So when Christ tells his disciples (Acts 1:8) that they shall receive *power* (*dunamis*) when the Holy Spirit comes upon them, he is saying that a dynamic new energy will flow into and through their lives.

The paradoxical aspect of experiencing the Holy Spirit as a force in your personality, is that you cannot make it happen. The experience is subject to the "Laws of Reverse Effect." The harder you try and the more you block that flow with your own Compliance, Criticalness, Helplessness, or Striving—the very partial perspectives we have discussed—the less you will experience. What you need to realize is that while God will love and accept and even work in a limited way through a partial personality, there is no good reason to remain partial and immature, or stuck, as we have called it.

If you want the Holy Spirit to flow freely in your life, you need to become a more whole personality. It takes maturity and balance to be able to allow the Spirit to flow through you unimpeded by personality distortions and rigidities. This, we suppose, is why a frustrated apostle wrote in Hebrews 5:12-14 (*KJV*), "For when for the time ye ought to be teachers, ye have need that one teach you again which be the first principles of the oracles of God; and are become such as have need of milk, and not of strong meat. For every one that useth milk is unskilful in the word of righteousness: for he is a babe. But strong meat belongeth to them that are of full age, even those who *by reason of use* have their senses *exercised* to discern both good and evil" (italics ours).

"Practice, practice, practice!" is a phrase we must emphasize again. We mean it. Laziness, drifting, superficial living, blind obedience, or arrogant self-assertion are all equally destructive to growth. Practice passionate prayer. Practice openness to how God communicates with you from day to day. Practice flexibility in learning new insights and refining old ones. Practice taking another point of view to stretch your empathy and understanding. Practice trusting your spontaneous responses in new situations. Practice asking God for help, affirmation, and the courage to be yourself. Practice asking other people for honest feedback about how you think, feel, and behave. Practice Scriptural directives other than your favorites. Practice stretching out on the personality polarities that we have described, especially those that seem most difficult or foreign to you. Practice, practice, practice—but most of all, learn from all the new things that happen! God is the originator of spontaneity and creativity, so you can flow most easily with his will by learning to expect and enjoy the surprises and serendipitous discoveries you find when you are in touch with him.

The paradox of personality growth is that we grow and change by accepting the way we are. We grow most when we relax and permit the Holy Spirit to inspire us from within and to help us shape outer circumstances as well. A relaxed faith in God, coupled with sincere desire for the Holy Spirit's guidance, allows our whole being time to assimilate new experiences, and gradually influences our values and behavior.

Jesus once said that human beings are like sheep. If we truly assimilate our experiences, then gradually the grass of the new learning will be transformed into the wool of wisdom that others can see and acknowledge.

The process of releasing the old and grasping the new is a natural part of Christian growth. Just as the trapeze artist must make his transition from one bar to the next, so the actualizing Christian must remain willing to depart from old ways in order to arrive at new ones. But God himself is a faithful part of the process. As Paul Tournier has said: "There is no strength greater than that of God to help us to let go of the past, and to escape from its bonds. But that past was in fact the strong support that God gave us to help us to leap forward towards him" (*A Place for You*, p. 201).

Time and again we must plunge beyond our manipulative relating patterns and partial perspectives into the stream of energy from the core. Jesus likened this stream of energy to "rivers of living water . . . this spake he of the Spirit, which they that believe on him should receive" (John 7:38, 39 KJV).

This active risking, trusting, and plunging reduces the influence of our defensive structures and opens up the flow of energy from the wellspring of God within our core. The core unifies the polarities of Love, Assertiveness, Weakness, and Strength, and heals the inner wounds of fear, releasing a flow of power that replaces *fear of life* with *faith in life*.

Elizabeth O'Connor has said that prayerful surrender to God from the core of one's being brings about a "fundamental change" in the quality of a person's life, so that life comes to be lived on an entirely different level. She writes:

Mysterious as this may sound, it actually has to do with changes in very ordinary aspects of living, such as increased awareness of what we see and hear, a heightened degree of receptivity, a growing capacity to respond—to be engaged in the moment as one who is fully present. (*Search for Silence*, p. 14)

Coming home to the core means learning to listen to the soft undertones of the Holy Spirit, which are noticeable in the depths of your personality and in your relationships with other people. King Solomon was aware of this when he wrote: "For wisdom and truth will enter the very center of your being, filling your life with joy" (Proverbs 2:10 TLB).

Living from this core, you, as an actualizing Christian, exemplify a new dimension of openness to life in the following ways. You become:

1. *An adventurer in truth.* You see Life as an adventure in becoming as whole as possible. You decide to learn from all that happens to you. Suppleness, plasticity, and—most important—the ability to profit from experience and education are required.

2. *An expressor of your own Christlikeness.* Because you learn to trust the Holy Spirit within, and to "pray without ceasing" for his inspiration, you gladly and thankfully go about developing the full repertoire of gifts, talents, ministries, and opportunities that God has placed within you.

3. *An enlightened traveler on the road of life.* Your core represents a light within. It is a light that each person must discover, and, once discovered, it becomes essential that you do not hide it under a bushel basket of shyness, fear, arrogance, or complacency. As a maturing Christian you can make your Spirit-inspired light shine so as to guide and encourage others to discover their inner light. As Jesus said, "You are the light of the world. . . . Let your light so shine before men, that they may see your good works and give glory to your Father who is in heaven" (Matthew 5:14, 16 RSV).

The kind of full and intimate companionship with God that we have been discussing may seem difficult to understand to some readers. Yet the message of the New Testament is that union with Christ by the power of the Holy Spirit is the calling of every Christian and the meaning of true spirituality. It then becomes highly feasible to speak of the inner core of the personality as being filled with the Holy Spirit. And the overflow of that "infilling" is a lifetime of graced relationships with others, as well as a steady stream of understanding and awareness about yourself.

One of the New Testament Greek words used for the Holy Spirit is *paraklētŏs*. This translates as "one called alongside to help," or "comforter," or "companion." These meanings clearly show a most personal and intimate role of the Holy Spirit in supporting, nurturing, teaching, and guiding a person through the journey of life.

Jesus promised the gift of the Holy Spirit to all who accepted and followed him (John 14:18). He portrayed the Holy Spirit as the believer's personal Companion, who would be adequate for all the needs of daily life. We encourage the reader who is unfamiliar with these references to read or reread the four Gospels, the book of Acts, and especially the Gospel of John, chapters 14 through 17.

As we move further toward integrating the Bible with depth psychology, we can say that the Holy Spirit is intended by God to be the *center* of our existence—the inspiration (from the Latin *inspirare,* meaning "to breathe into or upon") of our feelings, thoughts, values, and choices.

Some people are frightened by the idea of God's being so close to them because they suddenly feel self-conscious, as though they have to change a lot of things about themselves before he will really accept them. But actually the opposite is more true. Christ, through the Holy Spirit, is more humble in knocking at the human heart than we might ever suspect. We would expect such a man as Hitler and his storm troopers to catch us by surprise, convict us of our faults, and sentence us to a horrible existence. But God has no such thing in mind. The knock may be firm, especially if we are near the brink of self-destruction, but it is always respectful as well. And there is a smile on the face of this special Friend whenever we open our door. We do not have to be ashamed, we do not have to put everything in order, we do not have to pretend to be what we are not or make sudden desperate promises to reform.

Perhaps the most profound type of core experience a person can have comes in what it means to be "struck by grace." By grace we mean the *gift* of God that you are loved and accepted without effort on your part. Paul wrote, "For by grace are ye saved through faith; and that not of yourselves: it is the gift of God" (Ephesians 2:8 KJV). Theologian Paul Tillich describes the experience:

Do we know what it means to be struck by grace? . . . It happens; or it does not happen. . . . Grace strikes us when . . . we walk through the dark valley of a meaningless and empty life. It strikes us when we feel that our separation is deeper than usual. . . . It strikes us when our disgust for our own being, our indifference, our weakness, our hostility, and our lack of direction and composure have become intolerable to us. It strikes us when, year after year, the longed-for perfection of life does not appear . . . at that moment . . . it is as though a voice were saying: *You are accepted*, accepted by that which is greater than you . . . . After such an experience we may not be better than before, and we may not believe more than before. But everything is transformed. (*The Shaking of the Foundations*, pp. 161-62)

The center of healthy psychological and spiritual growth is the core, our innermost being. The core is not the raw, chaotic power of the unconscious that Freud portrayed. Rather, it is an innate guidance system that can be energized by the healing power of God's love. It is out of our core that dignity, courage, and love emerge so that we can live life to the fullest. The subtle promptings from the core enable us to become truly human, and to fulfill our unique missions in life.

The core can be understood as the home of divine support within the personality. Paul Tournier wrote in *A Place for You* (p. 200), "God is always there, always available, and for everyone, both small and great, unbelievers as well as believers, rebels as well as those who obey him."

With courage the maturing Christian recognizes within himself or herself the possibilities of manipulative living and personality disorder, or Spirit-led actualization. This is a humbling experience, but very appropriate. The creative tension that arises, owing to the Christian's desire to give in to the temporarily secure but self-defeating structures of Compliant, Critical, Helpless, or Striving life-styles on the one hand, and the desire to choose instead the more whole and life-enhancing integration of a Spirit-filled personality, makes every day a miracle of God's grace that augments one's deliberate decisions.

Søren Kierkegaard, the Danish philosopher, coined an apt term for what happens when we refuse the miracle. He said that a person begins to suffer the misery of "shut-upness." In shutting ourselves off from the unfolding adventure of a God-inspired universe, we begin gradually to lose touch with the deepest roots and potential of our lives.

But the Good News, the gospel, which Kierkegaard himself experienced, is that the universe is not a random event or a place devoid of meaning and purpose. In his *Journals* he wrote:

To have to say how I spend my time in prayer, how it is that I really live with God like father and son: that baring of myself, if I may so describe it, I find so difficult, so difficult; my inwardness is too true for me to be able to talk about it. (*The Journals of Kierkegaard*, ed. Alexander Dru, 1959, p. 165)

How profound a statement of what we all struggle with when it comes to letting God or others know what is really going on deep within us! Only the neurotic—the person safely encapsulated in the rigid confines of a personality disorder or partial expression of the self—knows the feeling of safety derived from hiding all or significant parts of the self. But that safe feeling is a pseudo-comfort, a shortcut, an avoidance, for which we subsequently pay a far greater, unaffordable price down the road of emptiness and depersonalization.

Perhaps the greatest of all sins is our unwillingness to open our hearts to Christ and his Holy Spirit, and to refuse to be open to people. Self-disclosure puts an end to pretense and replaces it with an authentic stand, whether this stand be our caring, our anger, our confidence, or our vulnerability. People need people. And each of us needs to practice openness, no matter how tentative, to the Lord. How else can God's healing love penetrate, communicate with, and touch us?

Author's personal comment—Ev:
I do acknowledge that I have a very strong and much tested faith in God's love for me and for humanity. But like every person, I have my moments of doubt, of confusion, of wondering what the rest of life will require from me.
Not so long ago I attended a communications workshop, mainly to keep up with the growing frontiers of my profession. Somehow, while reflecting on what transpired there, I became painfully aware that I had not

been completely honest about my feelings. I suppose this is a lifelong carryover from having been raised in a home where children were to be seen but not heard.

So I had become so busy telling my feelings what they should be that I refused to let them tell me what they actually were. I was so preoccupied socially with being a good psychologist that I denied people my own authenticity. I had been playing the role of psychologist, reeling off like a phonograph record the messages that had been recorded and drilled into me by those who trained me. But I had forgotten how to tell people how I really felt.

This experience, and discussing it with my wife was of great help to me, inspired me all the more to practice emotional self-expression, and to include this need for further growth as a vital part of my prayer agenda.

To be perfectly honest, awareness and discovery of this fault have occurred in cycles throughout my life, and now I recognize and value those cycles of learning as part of the Holy Spirit's ever present promptings to assist me in walking the walk, not just talking the talk, of a Christian life.

When I was twenty I thought I could do no wrong in living the Christian life. At thirty I wanted God's guidance to a degree, but only as far as it wouldn't interfere with my own plans. At forty, when my best seller, Man, the Manipulator, *was climbing the charts toward a million copies sold, I believed I had arrived. At fifty I began to discern that nobody "arrives"—that we all simply keep growing—if we remain open. At sixty I dedicated anew my life's work to whatever destiny God had planned for me when I was yet a babe. And at seventy or eighty, I believe I will feel satisfied simply to know that his healing love was patiently guiding me all along the way.*

That he touched me, and that he is still touching me is perhaps the most profound synopsis I can give of my life.

When we are blessed with grace through the Holy Spirit, we find ourselves loved and affirmed in such a way that we love God and others—we develop a tenderness toward existence. But the essential ingredient, which then becomes an irreversible aspect of our own core, is that such love is by nature unmerited—we are loved by God not because of our achievements or what we do. We are simply loved. And such love radiates outward to others in the same way.

Our spirituality is God's energy moving into and through our core. The core is the involuntary energy center into which flows the love of God and from which flows love for ourselves and others. As Paul says, "God's love has been poured into our hearts through the Holy Spirit" (Romans 5:5 RSV). Thus, love is expressed through the core, and love becomes central to our understanding of the core.

For anyone caught in the throes of disorientation, fear, or a sincere quest for meaning, the biblical principle "love casts out fear" is like a lighthouse in a stormy sea. It means that we are no longer lost or alone. Life can get pretty tough, but we can find our way home.

The Psalmist said—no doubt from personal experience and multiple crises: "I will lift up mine eyes unto the hills, from whence cometh my help. My help cometh from the Lord, which made heaven and earth" (Psalm 121:1-2 KJV).

EXERCISES

1. Take a little time to think back over moments in your life when fear and anxiety gripped you from within, and you found yourself floundering. These memories can still be charged with negative feelings that have the power to carry over into your perception of life as an adult. Make notes about several or even a dozen or

more of these negative experiences, and then discuss them with a trusted friend, a professional psychologist, a pastoral counselor, or someone who can offer deep insight and empathetic understanding to you. Remember, the memories and their continued impact on you will not go away on their own. Include God in the list of persons to whom you disclose painful memories. Also, watch for special seminars or church activities that focus on the theme, "healing of the memories." Most of all, do not be afraid of these memories anymore—no matter how bad or humiliating or embarrassing you think what happened to you was. Every human experience can be viewed in a larger context that can neutralize the toxic effects of that piece of past history. The therapeutic aim of working through past, disturbing or antigrowth experiences is to free you to use most of your energies to live creatively in the present and prepare wisely for the future. So regret, remorse, guilt, embarrassment, inhibition, or revenge with regard to past events does little good. You cannot rid yourself of memories, but you can choose to build constructively upon what you have learned, so that the same actions are never repeated, and also so that you can become a wiser person. The biggest point here is that you need to let the past die so that you can focus fully on your present potential.

2. How do you respond to Ashley Montagu's list of attributes for the growth-oriented person at any age? (see p. 138.) Do you agree or disagree? How many can you identify in your personality?

3. In the most important projects or relationships that you now have, ask for the gift of the Holy Spirit to augment your energies and amplify your talents. This

creates an expectation within you, so that you can anticipate and be open to the novel and surprising ways in which the Holy Spirit undergirds and inspires your efforts. Practice this discipline. Make it an adventure. Become curious about the outcome.

4. If there is one thing you would like to ask Jesus to help you with, what is it? If there is one trait in your personality you want very much to change, what is it? If there is one heart's desire that you would like God to help you to acquire, what is it? In the realm of answered prayer it is not so much the point to get things from God, as it is to spend time with and appreciate the Giver of all good things. The fact that the God of the Judeo-Christian faith takes real and personal interest in our lives means that we need to have sincere, heart-to-heart conversations with him often. How else can our relationship with him deepen and mature? To ask nothing is to receive nothing. To ask much and often is to create many opportunities for growth and learning to continue, both from the blessings that are received as well as from answers either temporarily or permanently withheld because of God's compassion and good judgment.

5. The next time you hear or sing the song, "Have thine own way, Lord! Have thine own way!/Thou art the potter; I am the clay," let go with your whole being to the experience of daring to release yourself to him. To be supple. To be flexible. To be daringly open to his promptings from within—and yet to be fully human and fallible every step of the way—this is the moment to moment way of life we advocate.

12

PERFECTION IS A PROCESS

Behold, the kingdom of God is within you.

—Jesus Christ

Your testimony as a growing Christian is not that you are perfect, but rather that you are being perfected by the love and power of God through Christ and the Holy Spirit.

How is it possible that the fear described in this book can be healed by the perfect love of God? We believe that the answer to this question is the knowledge that the actualizing Christian, in being filled and led by the Holy Spirit, lives in an atmosphere of inspiration rather than condemnation.

According to Webster's, to perfect means "to bring to final form." Our fears and stuckness are healed as we learn to actively trust the Holy Spirit to keep assisting our growth from within in every aspect of our lives. This is why we believe openness and relaxation are two primary traits that need to be cultivated in every Christian life.

Too many Christians are used to thinking in black and white terms, always labeling or pigeonholing every thought, feeling, or action as sinful or good, right or wrong. This type of thinking works well when a person is first born again spiritually, or as long as a person stays in an "elementary school of the Spirit." But it also leads to self-righteousness, needless tension, a judgmental approach to people, and a phoney sense of superiority. As a matter of fact, you can see this attitude most often in little children between ages six and nine, as they seek to understand and master "the rules" in order to avoid punishment and gain approval.

How often have you heard people say any of the following:

* Control yourself.
* Hold your temper—or you may harm somebody.
* Don't fall in love or you'll get hurt.
* Keep a level head.
* Don't let your emotions run away with you.

The truth is, we have all heard these pronouncements since we were old enough to understand what was being said around us. As a culture, we are obsessed with controls—both self-control and control by others. The popular notion in many Christian circles these days is that godly behavior is controlled behavior, that the spiritual person is the one who keeps a tight rein on his or her emotions. But we have yet to see a nervous breakdown that is not due to overcontrol, and to its aggravation by the nagging of friends and family to "pull yourself together."

The overcontrolled person behaves in exactly the same way as a fearful driver who drives with the brakes permanently on. The car has many controls. The brakes are just one of them, and the crudest of all. The better the driver understands how to handle all the controls, and how to be relaxed yet alert while driving, the more efficiently the car will function. But if he drives with brakes permanently on "just to be on the safe side," the wear and tear on the brake and engine will be enormous, the performance of the car will deteriorate, and sooner or later there will be a breakdown.

Most of us spend much of our lives "braking" ourselves. Why? Because we believed the people who told us that it is dangerous to let go. Behind this notion is a fear that unrestrained emotions have no limit, that unchecked, we will fly off into hysteria, blind rage, bottomless depression. But these behaviors are characteristic of the overcontrolled, not the controlled person.

As we have seen, we have many feelings and emotions that are constantly longing to be expressed. The unwillingness to experience and express one or more of them leads to manipulative behavior and a partial perspective about oneself and others. But what happens when we do allow ourselves full expression? Do we go on endless crying jags? Do we turn into raving lunatics? Do we become monsters? No. Because within each of us, there is a natural restraining function—a spiritual thermostat if you will. And how does a thermostat control temperature? If the temperature increases too much, the thermostat activates the air conditioner. If the temperature decreases too much, the thermostat activates the heat. If the temperature does not exceed in either direction the limits imposed, the thermostat does nothing.

Similarly, every Christian has a restraining function that is entirely internal, natural, and automatic—the Holy Spirit. Yet, how often we can overlook the presence of so valuable a Guest in favor of external control or manipulative overcontrol of our behavior and the behavior of others.

One way to see ourselves is as a dynamic, everchanging "organism," bipolar in its potential for expression. The picture that comes to mind is that of a teeter-totter, the child's playground toy made up of a long board, which is suspended by a fulcrum in the middle. If we label one end "liberal," to describe our open, uninhibited, expressive side, and the other end "conservative," to describe our cautious, traditional, controlled side, the teeter-totter resembles figure 9.

As any child knows, when the two sides of the teeter-totter are balanced, it swings gently up and down, up and down, with one side counterbalancing the movement of the other. In the same way, when we are balanced, our teeter-totter moves continually in dynamic interplay between our liberal and conservative potentials.

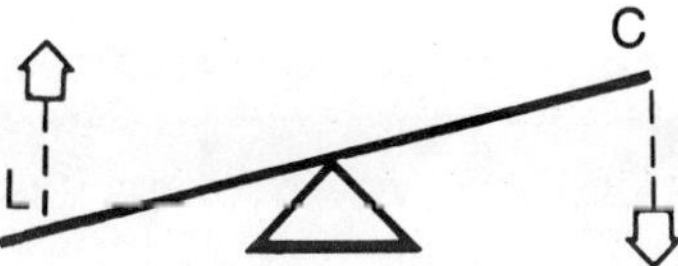

Fig. 9   LIBERAL/CONSERVATIVE TEETER-TOTTER

One end of the teeter-totter rises, and our awareness of the needs of that side of our nature predominates. Circumstances change, and the other end of the teeter-totter rises. As long as we continue to live by the LAWS of expression—expressing what we feel in our core through an appropriate polarity—then we will continue to move in organismic balance. Neither the liberal nor the conservative ends will become fixed and dominate our personality.

But when our balance is artificially upset, the result is loss of movement, loss of action, loss of "life." This is the beginning of a partial perspective that can be rigidified even more into a specific pattern of manipulative behavior and on into a personality disorder. What has been lost in order to gain the security of total predictability? Gracefulness, ease of expression, and adventure have been traded for perpetual, static sameness.

Whether the disruption of organismic self-trust is caused by you or simply allowed to happen by you, the responsibility for the loss of aliveness rests within you. And the courage required to do whatever you have to do to restore trust in your core and to renew the flow of your real feelings lies within you as well. To be a person, or to be a statue—that is the question. You must take responsibility for the situation and determine whether your being and personality are to be static and fixed or dynamic and rhythmic.

Responsibility in this sense means accepting that you are the cause of your own natural rhythmic balance; you are not dependent on anyone else to establish controls for your behavior. Thus, to say, "I won't physically hurt another because there are laws against it," is an abdication from this responsibility. On the other hand, it is an acceptance of responsibility to say, "I'm so angry, I want to hurt somebody, but I know that doing it will not alleviate my anger; besides, it's not productive and it just makes matters worse."

Here the "liberal" end got an opportunity to express itself, and the "conservative" end was able to temper the expression with logic and restraint. A spiritually wise solution presented itself through the free interplay of both sides.

We all have liberal and conservative sides; each side must accept the existence and role of the other. In the open acceptance and expression of both sides of our nature, we have a natural means by which to live our lives with the greatest inspiration and ease. This still affords us an abundance of challenges, but with a minimum of artificial controls imposed from without.

External morality systems are artificial control devices, which some of us believe are required to keep immature people from behaving unwisely. As parents and spouses, we feel the need to impose such systems on our children and mates because, deep down, we do not trust our own organismic balance and therefore we cannot trust the balance of those we love. But, as Christians, isn't this a statement of our lack of real trust in the Holy Spirit, who inhabits our minds, hearts, and bodies; the One about whom we may speak eloquently, while nevertheless refusing to acknowledge as present in the depths of our being?

Another way to view the natural restraining function is as a series of figure eights (see figure 10). There we see all of the basic polarities, along with the intensity levels of each. Because of the natural restraining function, when we experience one of these polarities, especially at the higher levels of intensity, what follows next is not necessarily more of the same. As with the teeter-totter, what follows is more likely to be an experience of the opposite polarity.

How often have you heard someone say, "I laughed until I cried," or "Our lovemaking is always most intense after we have had a big fight," or "Just when I'd given up trying, I suddenly found new strength to start again," or "I feel so much better now that I've gotten that off my chest." This is not an unusual or unnatural phenomenon. In fact, it's perfectly natural and predictable. Do not condemn yourself for loving somebody deeply one moment and being furious with him or her the next. In such instances, your natural restraining function is simply inhibiting you from flying off too far in just one direction. So relax and do not try to stifle or control it.

We recommend that you indelibly imprint figure 10 in your memory so that you can refer to it often and at needed times throughout life. In years of teaching, group work, and working with thousands individually, we have found this simple diagram to be of immense value to every individual who has mastered it.

Immediately you recognize the familiar "compass points of the self" format. But now we have categorized the inner portions of each polarity with ranges of intensity. For instance, on the Love polarity the first impression we usually feel upon meeting someone is in the range of "interest." Only after a variety of positive experiences with this person over a period of time will the initial positive impression of interest expand to a greater intensity, "attraction." As time goes on, and more positive experiences are shared, the range of intensity becomes "caring." Finally, if the relationship has a good track record and the person comes to be regarded as a very special part of our lives, our feelings rise still further, and the intensity range becomes "tender caring."

The same principle holds true for each of the polarities, and we need to become emotionally mature and spiritually centered enough to take responsibility for these degrees of involvement so that we know at any given time just what is happening in each relationship we have. By becoming aware of our real feelings, and through developing active skills for communicating them accurately and honestly, our lives acquire a much sharper focus—a clearer in-depth grasp of the nature and intensity of each relationship. *Knowledge* of the theory is the first key. *Awareness* of how it works in your life is the second. *Experimentation* with improving the quality of every relationship is the third. Continual practice and

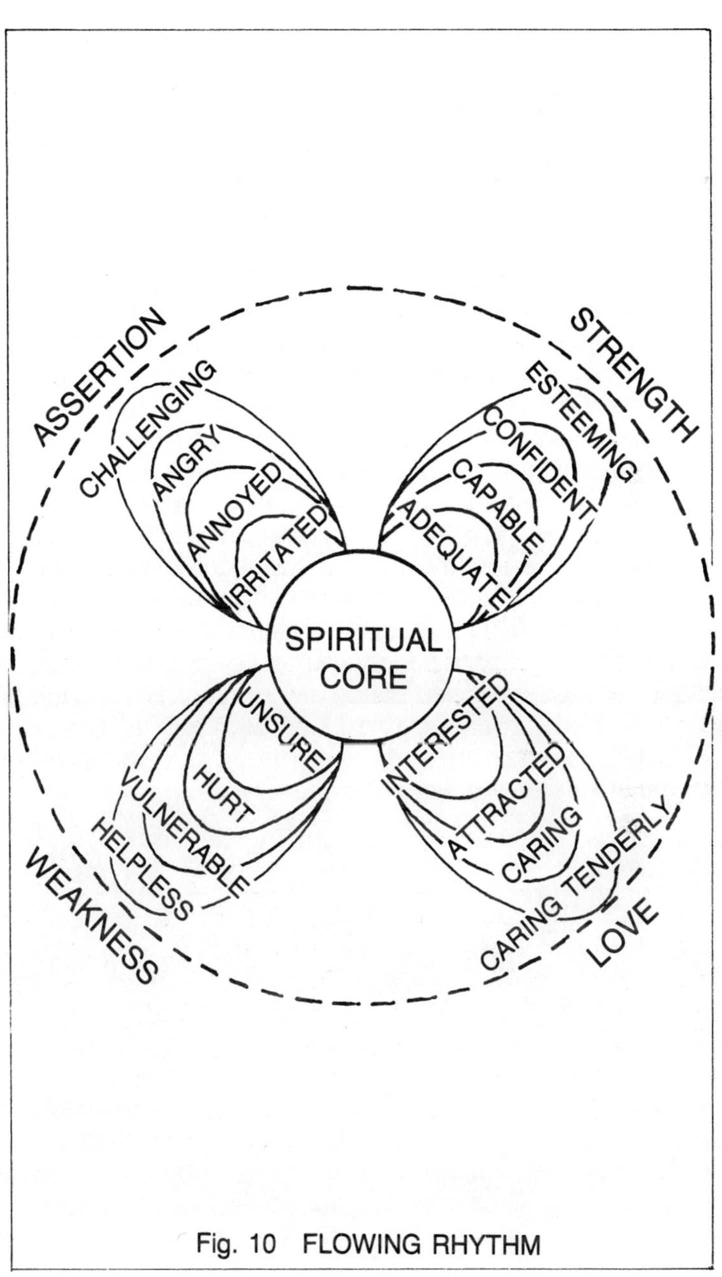

Fig. 10   FLOWING RHYTHM

mastery of these LAWS of personality is the fourth. And developing a deep *openness* to the Holy Spirit for guidance in every aspect of healthy relating—as well as in the art of neutralizing the effects of toxic or unhealthy relationships—is the last.

With awareness, prayer, and gentle discipline, the partial perspectives we may be stuck in are gradually transformed into stages of growth—like the bud that eventually blossoms into a flower, the opening petals of which are symbolic of the LAWS in figure 10. If someone impatiently tries to tear the covering of the bud away, the flower inside can be destroyed. In the same way, we need to respect the slow and gradual transformation of our constricted personality into a fully alive and expressive one.

With courage, growing Christians recognize within themselves the possibility of rigidification into personality disorders or inspiration into Spirit-filled actualization. It is the potential for either personality disorder or actualizing that makes each day, each month, each year a time of creative choice between personal surrender to the miracle of God's grace or a resistant stand against it.

We like the understanding that theologian Theodore Runyon brings to this issue:

Because God values and respects our human freedom, the presence of his Spirit may be ignored or overlooked or buried beneath years of insensitivity and indifference. . . . Jesus never imposes himself on anyone. He meticulously honors the right of people to turn away from him as well as toward him, because his reign is not something that can be imposed but must be freely willed by anyone who would be his follower. (*What the Spirit Is Saying to the Churches*, p. 14)

The Holy Spirit can be understood to come from within the personality much as a seed is placed within fertile soil. The Spirit is like a mustard seed that grows within, as opposed to a mustard plaster slapped on from without.

There is real wisdom built into the human personality. It is as though God intended the inner core to prompt us through a sensitive set of checks and balances in order to create a reliable source of guidance and inspiration within each person—a "law written upon their hearts."

Love that is fully expressed brings qualities of tenderness, caring, and nurture into the world. However, to have its finest balance, love must be offset with Assertiveness. Assertion creates boldness to confront the world in a caring way. Likewise, the feelings of Strength and Weakness both balance and check each other. From Strength a person derives confidence, dignity, and self-esteem. But with the balancing effect of Weakness, the virtue of empathy is added. As a result a person can express strength without becoming arrogant, and still remain open to the feelings and opinions of others.

The back and forth movement from one polarity of feelings to another is what makes personality dynamic. A feeling can be defined as a person's private, emotionally colored perception of self, others, or the world at any given moment. That perception is not necessarily accurate or realistic, but it is there; it represents that person's subjective reality at a particular moment. That is why our feelings reveal the truth about ourselves, and why we need to become so aware of them.

If you want to know the truth about how someone views or responds to any situation, you must ask them how they feel. Feelings are the energy of personality, and without them we become boring and colorless. By becoming aware of our feelings, especially ones we have repressed or inhibited, we can learn to channel the energy of personality into the world in positive ways.

One of the biggest challenges of the Christian life is to transform the hurts, pains, and frustrations we all experience into a growth process that contributes to our maturity in the Lord.

Author's personal comment—Dan:
An African Christian, who had suffered the loss of his family in the massacre of Leopoldville, once told me that a Christian is like a rose. God allows the bad and painful experiences of life to act as fertilizer. In so doing, he neutralizes the poisonous effects of pain, and actually makes it serve his purposes by transforming it into beauty.

Often as Christians we believe that the sooner we get rid of our pain and put on a smiling, victorious face, the sooner we will get back on the track of God's will. However, this approach tends to do the exact opposite. For in our desire to act as though we feel fine or as though we have great faith, we in fact must repress or hide our deep inner feelings of pain. In so doing, we lose touch with ourselves, and we also lose our sensitivity to what God is trying to teach us through the process of genuine suffering and dawning awareness.

The task of the rose is not to pretend that the fertilizer is not there, or to get rid of the fertilizer by absorbing it all at once. Rather, when fertilizer has been administered to the rose by the helpful gardener, the rose must simply be patient enough to allow some days and even weeks to pass while the fertilizer is drawn up through the roots into the rose's life and gradually assimilated.

The fertilizer is profoundly changed. It loses its nature as a poisonous and foul-smelling waste. It becomes the rose itself. The dung becomes the delicate and fragrant blooms of the growing plant.

Authentic pain or suffering—that is, pain or suffering not brought about by our own neurotic attitudes—is often the precursor of genuine insight and change, change we need to be thankful for, because without it our limitations would overtake our potentials like weeds running wild in a potentially beautiful garden.

The maturing Christian learns to integrate many

apparent opposites. Openness to experience all that you are without the need to be defensive, repressive, or apologetic can be expressed as follows:

I am neither good nor bad, I am both.
I am neither spiritual nor sensual, I am both.
I am neither generous nor selfish, I am both.
I am neither saint nor sinner, I am both.
But God accepts me, forgives me, and loves me just as I am.
And I can accept, forgive, and love myself and others.
(Cecil Osborne, *The Art of Learning to Love Yourself*)

The process of becoming a born-again Christian involves a decision to open yourself to the forgiveness of Christ and the inspiration of the Holy Spirit. After that, your task as a Christian is to accept and utilize the growth process of moving from the childlikeness of the new born Christian to the discerning depths and wholeness of a gradually maturing, Spirit-filled personality.

The actualizing Christian seeks to integrate the childlike qualities of openness to experience, freshness of perception, and excitement for living, with the more adult qualities of knowing the consequences of our behavior and sensitive discipline in what we say and do. We learn to "pray without ceasing," as Paul would say, because we sense very deeply our reliance upon God to assist us in every way, in every moment of life. But our prayer is relaxed, because we understand that it is our hearts that God wants to capture—not the technicality of how well or often we pray. As someone once said, "it is not our ability or inability that impresses God, but rather our *availability* that counts."

This is the surrender we have been talking of. This is the openness of one's whole being and personality to the unfolding, dynamic will of God. We do not believe that it is a once-and-for-all event as much as it is a continuous affirmation and adventure.

As we focus our energies on becoming truly Christ-like—able to love God, ourselves, and others as purely as he loves us—the Holy Spirit augments our natural efforts by gracing us with appropriate and special gifts and talents. Paul expands this principle in 1 Corinthians (12:4-6, 11 *TLB*) as follows:

Now God gives us many kinds of special abilities, but it is the same Holy Spirit who is the source of them all. There are different kinds of service to God, but it is the same Lord we are serving. There are many ways in which God works in our lives, but it is the same God who does the work in and through all of us who are his. . . . It is the same and only Holy Spirit who gives all these gifts and powers, deciding which each one of us should have.

Growth never happens overnight, any more than a plant or a baby can grow to full stature overnight. Growth is a lifetime process. Therefore, we need to become very patient with both ourselves and others, at whatever stage of growth we are undergoing. On the other hand, we need to be vigilant and alert as well, so that we do not miss the special opportunities for growth that God continually brings to us. What we need are the paradoxical qualities of relaxed alertness, prudent openness, and gentle discipline to make the best progress through life.

The dove is one of the biblical symbols for the Holy Spirit (see figure 2), because the Spirit reveals his wisdom and love through gentleness like that of the dove. It does not facilitate the quiet and gradual work of the Spirit in our lives if we approach growth in a tense, perfectionistic, legalistic, and tight-jawed manner; nor, by contrast, if we are too lax. This is why it is so important to learn to serve the Lord out of love and creativity rather than out of fear and rigidity.

All the essential elements for a Spirit-filled life-style are already in our personalities. Nothing needs to be added or taken away—just filled out, balanced, and fine-tuned.

EXERCISES

1. How do you respond to our statement that it is better "to serve the Lord out of love and creativity than out of fear and rigidity"? Looking at your own relationship with Christ, how free do you feel to follow his guidance through daily and weekly inspiration as opposed to fearfully trying to please him? Why or why not?

2. Do you personally identify with the model of "instant perfection" or "growth over time" in your spiritual life?

3. Is your perception of God one of a stern, demanding Father, or an empathetic, understanding, and supportive Friend?

4. Can you muster the courage to integrate your pains, betrayals, disappointments, and hurts—and still find a special bit of courage to remain receptive to what life may be teaching you, and to stay open to the plan God has for your life?

5. Are you mature enough to accept both the hardships and the miraculous moments of life—as well as to stretch yourself into being open with and even trusting of God in all things? Are you integrating the following scripture into your personal orientation to life: "For it is God which worketh in you both to will and to do of his good pleasure" (Philippians 2:13 *KJV*)?

13

THE SPIRIT-FILLED PERSONALITY

We are empty vessels to be filled by the Lord. To be filled with the life of Jesus in accordance with who we deeply are is the Christian definition of self-fulfillment.

—Adrian van Kaam

The love end of the Love/Assertion polarity is expressed verbally with phrases such as "I'm interested," "I'm attracted," "I care," and "I care tenderly." The actualizing Christian has access to the effective experience and expression of all these intensities of love.

Examine your own life for a minute. Can you verbally say to family and friends: "I love you"? Can you sort out in your own mind the various kinds of love that you feel? If you know how to say the words, can you back them up with concrete actions as well as physical expressions such as a hug, a pat on the shoulder, a wink, a smile, and a thoughtful touch? This is what Paul was getting at in his phrase: "Greet all the brethren with an holy kiss" (1 Thessalonians 5:26 KJV).

Now, admittedly, kissing has entirely different connotations in twentieth-century life and culture. But what he is really saying is "Touch each other—make physical contact that conveys caring, understanding, and support." (See film by Ashley Montagu, "Touching," available through Psychological and Educational Films,

3334 East Coast Hwy., #252, Corona Del Mar, CA 92625. A list of twelve films relating to actualizing is included in the Appendix.) This puts us in a bind in western culture, because touching tenderly is generally restricted to mean "I am sexually interested in you." But the individual who masters the LAWS of personality learns to separate physical touching from erotic encounter. A tender touch is part of the concrete expression of the Love polarity, and therefore the person who truly understands this can use his or her body as a means to express warm concern to a relative, a child, a spouse, or even a stranger, without overtones of sexual desire. Grace Stuart explains in a passage from *Narcissus:* "We want to touch . . . and a culture that has placed a taboo on tenderness leaves us stroking dogs and cats when we may not stroke each other. We want to be touched . . . and often we dare not say so. . . . We are starved for the laying on of hands."

Over the past decade the charismatic or pentecostal movements in both Protestant and Catholic segments of the church have seemingly revived and emphasized the importance of emotional and physical touching. Any excesses or confusions brought along in the wake of these new directions do not negate the rediscovery that religion needs to be personally felt in body and mind, and that this experience likewise needs to be conveyed to others. How graphically the apostle John captured the need and reality of physical validation when he wrote: "We are writing to you about the Word of Life: He was from the beginning; we have heard Him, we have seen Him with our eyes, we have looked at Him, and our hands have touched Him" (1 John 1:1 MLB).

Love without touch is abstract. Touch without love is seductive. Love with touch is concrete—it crosses the gap between physically isolated human beings with an energy that can be felt and understood.

Likewise, verbalization of love is profoundly important. How many times have we heard in our counseling sessions that a hurting spouse or an alienated child never heard the words: "I love you."

In Keith Miller's book, *Please Love Me,* the protagonist, Hedy Robinson, asks the stirring question:

I couldn't help wondering if there weren't families somewhere in which people told each other every day about the love they felt and hugged and kissed each other—where people shared their hopes and dreams, their difficulties and fears at the dining room table. I tried to imagine our doing that, but couldn't. As long as I could remember, I'd wanted to express my feelings of love and affection to people close to me. But the greater fear of being rejected always kept me from it. (Waco, Tex.: Word Books, 1977, p. 66)

Author's personal comment—Ev:
My dad was raised in the old school of Scandinavian thinking, where sentimentality or emotion was viewed as a personal weakness, and a man was taught to rule his home with an iron fist.

I can't tell you how many times as a youngster I longed to be hugged and cuddled and told I was loved. But none of this was in my father's scope of behavior.

I was taught to control my behavior through fear of his authority and judgment, but never to expect his love through tenderness or warmth.

At forty years of age I finally had had enough inner pain and frustration to dare to confront him with my need for his love. Courage overcame my deep anxiety as one day I yelled at him, "Why don't you love me?" He was extremely offended by my question and immediately left the room, a raging scowl upon his face.

I ran after him into the next room. "It's true," I shouted. "You've always held me at a distance—and I need *your love! And now you're doing what you've always done—walking out on me when I need you the most." I felt extremely angry, and no longer shy at this moment.*

He turned slowly to face me. Then his stern face melted and tears filled his eyes. He reached out his arms and I filled them. Voice choking, he whispered, "I never knew how, son . . . I never knew how to love you."

We walked out of that bedroom that day united as never before. I now knew my father loved me, because he had finally shown me. I forgave him immediately. To this day, and he has been dead for many years, I have a real sense of closeness to him, a sense that would not have been possible without our mutual risk and reaching out for each other.

Love not expressed is love lost. Love released is love that can be felt and understood. And to feel loved is one of the greatest experiences a human being can know.

But just as valuable as love for shaping and defining a human life, Assertion allows each of us to acknowledge our individual differences, even while affirming our emotional and spiritual connection. The assertion end of the Love/Assertion polarity can be expressed at lower levels as "I feel irritated (or annoyed)." At higher levels of intensity, direct confrontation or challenging may be appropriate. Notice that the intensity of feeling increases as you move from the early stages of assertion—"I'm irritated"—to the most intense stage of assertion—"I challenge that (or you)."

All people feel angry from time to time. It is a natural and important feeling. Human beings are like sandpaper, and when we rub each other the wrong way, we need to say, "Ouch," or "I resent that." Diplomatic confrontation often makes open anger unnecessary.

Anger that is not honestly acknowledged or expressed comes out in subconscious and destructive ways. For instance, the man who gets mad at his boss, but keeps smiling in order not to rock the boat, may go home and yell at his wife over some trivial event. The wife may then displace her anger onto the children, who may in their turn kick the dog. All this displacement causes confusion, hurt feelings, and no constructive awareness for anyone. On top of this, the original unresolved situation with the boss will not change magically. Rather, it will fester like an infected sore, causing even greater annoyance.

For the actualizing Christian, anger or irritation are expressed as responsible self-assertion. The best way to integrate the assertion polarity with many or most of your relationships is to "agree to disagree" at times—to give each other space to be loyal to individual views while still being loyal to the relationship.

Holding in anger creates spitefulness, passive-aggressive behavior, discontent, brooding, and even a wrathful spirit. Expressing anger diplomatically and effectively requires great maturity and much practice. Anger is one of the most volatile of human emotions, and should be treated with great care and sensitivity. Too much or too little anger expressed can wreck marriages, confuse one's children, ruin partnerships, alienate bosses or subordinates, and distort personality.

The principle that can guide you in this avenue of self-expression can best be summed up as: any feeling, especially anger or irritation, which persists over time in a relationship that you care about, needs to be expressed. Rather than allowing unexpressed resentment to build walls between you and someone you care for, risk letting it out—but do so as diplomatically as possible, so as not to destroy the relationship or polarize the other person against you. Other people have their viewpoint too. And if your expression of anger does not in the end give way to a new openness to their feelings and perceptions, then most likely you have gone too far, and an apology may be in order.

Assertiveness is not meant to break down relationships, or to allow the irresponsible discharge of negative feelings, but to create understanding and reconciliation out of temporary alienation. Anger and assertiveness should always force us into a deeper understanding of our own motives, needs, and biases, and cause us to turn controversy into compromise.

A beautiful example from the New Testament (in the book of Acts) shows how the original disciples felt irritated, angered, and threatened by the announcement that the formerly zealous persecutor of Christians, Saul of Tarsus, now himself claimed to have encountered Jesus and desired to become a devoted preacher and teacher of the Christian faith. But that initial doubt, resentment, and skepticism gradually gave way to a new trust and understanding—and Paul was finally accepted into the inner circle of those who knew Jesus intimately.

In this example confrontation gave way to new insight—angry dispute became fertile soil for new understanding. This corroborates our own clinical experience that most always neither party is perfectly right in any argument or dispute. More often than not, both parties need to find a greater synthesis of truth by transcending the original dispute—no matter what that might be—and coming to a greater scope of understanding.

The more pertinent guideline for experiencing and expressing assertion or anger is to do so on a "cash and carry" and "open-ended" basis. It is far better to "be . . . angry, and sin not: let not the sun go down upon your wrath" (Ephesians 4:26 *kjv*), than to hold anger secretly within your heart or to blast someone with both barrels of double-ought shot because you disagree with them.

Modulation of self-expression (that is, expressing first awareness of feelings rather than letting them build to volatile proportions) and an openness to the rhythmic swings in feeling that follow authentic expression (that is, tender feelings often following the assertion of anger in a relationship you really care about) are principles which exemplify our whole theory.

Adding to the synthesis and rhythmic flow of Love and Assertion, we now turn to a similar figure-eight rhythm between Weakness and Strength.

In American culture there is a taboo against weakness and vulnerability, especially for men. Seldom can we afford to express such phrases as "I am unsure," "I feel vulnerable," "I feel hurt," or "I feel helpless" (see figure 10). And yet we all have these feelings from time to time. We all feel anxious, scared, helpless, or weak.

In our culture, where competition, individuality, and performance reign supreme, it is no surprise that any sense of weakness is repressed from awareness. Yet, when a part of us that is quite real is pushed out of consciousness, we are more vulnerable than ever because we lose touch with our core being. Our energies are diverted to present a false self—an idealized image—to the world. We may even believe that this ideal self—se-cure, flawless, and capable in all situations—is our real self. This kind of vanity is the real target of the scriptural "pride goeth before destruction" (Proverbs 16:18 *KJV*).

Whether it was Clark Gable, Humphrey Bogart, Jimmy Dean, or Paul Newman, men were never allowed to cry on the big screen of the local theater. And when women cried, they became hysterical and desperately helpless, and were usually slapped by the male hero to bring them to their senses. How unfortunate that men's and women's roles became so rigid and distorted.

From our view every man, woman, and child on the planet has the right to feel hurt, helpless, and frustrated at times, and to express that feeling authentically through talking or tears. Anything else is a cover-up and leads to nothing but confusion and pretense.

When it comes to being a person—a real mixture of confidence and insecurity, of strength and weakness—the distinction between men and women needs to fade into the background so that the real feelings of the person can come to the fore. How else can people communicate genuine feelings and needs?

The maturing Christian needs to learn to experience directly and without pretense the occasional hurts and disappointments of life. There are many little hurts from day to day that are real and painful. A sharp word from a spouse, a disappointment over a shattered hope, or an unfortunate misunderstanding with a friend can wound feelings. If these wounds are not allowed into awareness, we may become irritable, restless, or depressed later in the day—all "cover-up" reactions to the real and original feeling of weakness.

Only by becoming aware, as soon as possible, of the primary feeling of hurt can we do something constructive about it. We can confront the person who from our view caused the wound. We can decide that we are being too touchy and thin-skinned and work on learning how to handle a degree of criticism without going to pieces over it. We can share the hurting feeling with another person or a trusted friend. Or we can use the disappointment to remind ourselves that there are truly no guarantees in life—to choose to love and care for others is always a risk; we can therefore live like a hermit crab in a protective shell, or accept the challenge of learning to handle the sometimes ecstacy and sometimes agony that life brings.

Author's personal comment—Dan:
In the fifth grade I fell in love with Judy Simpson. I could hardly concentrate on anything elese.

That winter the New Mexico sky unloaded its powdery snow, and Third Street where I lived became the choice hill for rendezvous of dozens of kids.

My sled scooted like a racecar. Looking back on those happy moments I still cringe at what happened next—I think of it now as a sort of an initation into a world where there is about as much evil as there is good.

My last time of careening down the hill I landed at the feet of a group of boys who quickly formed a circle around me. Only one of the faces did I recognize, and it was he who emerged from the ring like a prize fighter, fists up and moving in a hypnotic fashion. Larry could draw animals better than anybody in fifth grade. Why was he waving his fists at me?

Suddenly blows exploded all over my chilled face. Blood spurted everywhere. I picked myself up off the ice and fists rained down on me again. I collapsed into darkness and pain, and when revived, found myself at home with anxious parents sponging dirt and blood out of deep cuts in my face.

Is terror the word I should use? I had been exploited in the cruelest way to satisy Larry's need for prestige and power—betrayed because we had even been friends up to now. But the worst came the next day.

Word passed like a prairie fire that Larry had beaten up Dan. And Judy found a new boyfriend by three o'clock that afternoon.

Now if my theory as a psychologist is that pain can be transformed into growth, and that weakness is as important a personal experience as strength, then you have the right to wonder what good I possibly got out of this humiliating experience of personal helplessness and hurt.

The growth did not come easily, but it did come. Whoever said that life is a rose garden was only half right. Roses can be made to bloom, but they can also become a crown of thorns for one to wear. Being badly beaten up by Larry at a tender age stimulated what has become one of my greatest gifts to people: empathy. Empathy is the capacity to feel another person's pain, to somehow identify with their suffering in a caring way. My start on my life's mission to make sense of people's pain and to encourage growth no matter what barriers stand in the way began the day I fell to the ground at Larry's feet.

The experience of hurt and vulnerability can also lead us closer to the Lord, who himself experienced misunderstandings, disappointments, and hard times. To see some of the very real ways that Jesus suffered psychological and emotional pain consider the following scriptures (KJV): In Matthew 26:38 he was "exceeding sorrowful"; in John 11:33 he "groaned in the spirit"; in Mark 3:5 he was "grieved"; in John 12:27 he was "troubled"; in John 11:35 he "wept"; and in Hebrews 5:7 he prayed with "strong crying and tears."

Paul was well acquainted with the reality of the Weakness polarity. He wrote: "For the sake of Christ . . . I am content with weaknesses, insults, hardships, persecutions, and calamities; for when I am weak, then I am strong" (2 Corinthians 12:10 RSV). In Christ we find a Friend who empathizes with our deepest hurts and, with his understanding, restores hope and courage to our lives.

Out of accepting and constructively utilizing weakness and emotional pain, the growing Christian emerges from the situation with self-esteem and strength intact. The deep and abiding source of that courage is not human nature, but God—yet the facilitators of healing and restoration of self-confidence are most often God's chosen channels, people.

Weakness and vulnerability are occasions to draw near to God or to a trusted friend for comfort, guidance, and encouragement. The old Christian hymn by Charlotte Elliott seems to say it well:

> Just as I am, without one plea,
> But that thy blood was shed for me,
> And that thou bidst me come to thee,
> O Lamb of God, I come, I come!
>
> Just as I am, though tossed about
> With many a conflict, many a doubt,
> Fightings and fears within, without,
> O Lamb of God, I come, I come!

A more profound expression of hurt and vulnerability is grief. Grief occurs when a person experiences a loss that strikes so deeply as to cause him or her to feel "brokenhearted." Perhaps a marriage has been abruptly ended. Perhaps there has been a tragic accident that has destroyed one's health or property. Perhaps someone has died—a parent, spouse, child, or dearest friend.

In the solitude of grieving, you need to find courage to trust the God-given emotional and physiological processes that allow for full catharsis of inner pain—crying, moaning, trembling, sleepless nights, or temporary hopelessness. You can trust the grieving process as surely as you know that nighttime eventually gives way to a new day. Anne Morrow Lindbergh has described the importance of vulnerability in being human: "Grief is a great leveler. . . . To grow, to be reborn, one must remain vulnerable—open to love but also hideously open to the possibility of more suffering" (*Hour of Gold, Hour of Lead*, p. 215).

And to show us how closely God himself identifies with our sufferings, we have that most intriguing verse found in Romans (8:26 *MLB*): "The Spirit joins in to help us in our weakness; for we do not know what and how we ought to pray, but the Spirit Himself intercedes on our behalf with sighs too deep for words."

When we are able to give in to and then come to

emotional closure on feelings of pain or hurt, we become able to see things in a new light. We can finally accept reality, and no longer upset ourselves with what is. Having given up our fanatical grasp of "how things should have been," we now regain touch with events, relationships, and opportunities that are currently shaping our lives. By gaining closure on what is in the past, the past with its bad memories and unrequited dreams loses its hold on us—we become free to live in the present, in the here and now, where we can, with God's assistance, rediscover the adventure of living.

The final polarity we want to enlarge upon is Strength. One way to tell almost immediately if you have difficulty in this area, is by whether or not you can accept and enjoy compliments that are given to you. If you can take in and feel warmed by someone's admiration or appreciation of your personality or your work, then chances are good that you already understand what the Strength polarity is all about. But if you somehow devalue or discount the incoming praise, you have not yet learned how great you truly are, through God's grace.

As we have said before, we are all fallible (fall-able) human beings on a journey of growth throughout this life. The perfection that is at work in our inner cores comes from God's perfect love through Christ and the Holy Spirit; it is not our own. We are gradually perfected—that is, made whole in every way—but the process will only be consummated in the life to come.

Rightly understood, this insight is extremely powerful because it helps us to know that we need not pretend to be more or greater than we really are. Our testimony is not that we are perfect, but that we have encountered the Redeemer—the One who forgives and accepts us right here and right now.

The attitude of perfectionism was the psychological disorder that so angered Christ in many of the Pharisees he met. They had no humility, no inner sense of a personal need for God's grace, forgiveness, and guidance. They thought that their own rituals, status, and routine prayers were enough to impress both man and God. They were wrong. Perfectionism leads to self-righteousness, that "holier than thou" attitude that turns people into judges and faultfinders rather than healers and empathizers.

But for people who would humble themselves before God and man—you and me provided we give up the façade of always being right or always perfect—for the humble of heart grace abounds, and God himself takes pleasure in affirming their greatness. For "God resisteth the proud, but giveth grace unto the humble" (James 4:6 KJV).

The whole point of humility—or freely acknowledging your human imperfection—is to gain immediate access to God's love and your own sense of self-esteem.

The Bible is clear that the kingdom of God need not begin only when we arrive at heaven. Rather, the kingdom of God has already burst into time and space and history (George Eldon Ladd, *A Theology of the New Testament*, p. 551). The more we live from our cores, the more we experience the gracious powers of the kingdom of God—here and now. So the actualizing Christian has hope not only for a blessed eternity, but also for substantial healing, meaning, and fulfillment in this life, as Francis Schaeffer has pointed out (in *True Spirituality*).

Many Christians are not sufficiently aware of this exciting prospect. An example is a marine sergeant who was recently talking to Dan. He confided sincerely that he was afraid to make a deep commitment to Christ because he felt he could not handle the new obligation to straighten out his life and give up some bad habits he enjoyed. "If I surrender to God, he will judge me and send me to some remote corner of the earth," he said. Dan suggested that the whole meaning of the death and resurrection of Christ was that God loves each one of us perfectly, that "God sent not his Son into the world to condemn the world; but that the world through him might be saved" (John 3:17 *KJV*). So why would such a loving God want to make Jim miserable?

God sent Jesus into the world to liberate people, not to condemn and frustrate them. Jim had never seen that side of it, but had rather assumed that God was the kind of gruff and stern Being with whom one ought not to get too intimate, rather like an intimidating marine sergeant!

The Bible presents an altogether different picture of God and the believer. Just as God gives his glory to Christ, Jesus gives his glory to the Christian (John 17:22). The actualizing Christian discovers this and feels gratitude, strength, and joy. As in figure 10, you can verbalize this gratitude by such Holy Spirit inspired soliloquies as "I am adequate," "I am capable," "I am confident," and "I am worthwhile." The awareness of your strengths, gifts, talents, and calling become a vital part of self-esteem.

Sensing your strengths is reflected in an unpretentious kind of self-confidence. Because you know that all genuine strength is rooted in the grace of God, you share God's serenity about it. The Psalmist expressed it this way: "He is like a tree planted by streams of water, that yields its fruit in its season, and its leaf does not wither. In all that he does, he prospers" (Psalm 1:3 *RSV*).

You as a Christian may do great things in the world, receiving much attention and acclaim, or you may quietly be great in ordinary ways. But your magnanimity, if it is genuine, will not appear to others arrogant, self-conscious, or forced. You will learn to know in every cell of your body and every corner of your mind what Zechariah discovered when he was compelled to write, " 'Not by might, nor by power, but by my Spirit,' says the Lord" (Zechariah 4:6 *RSV*).

A key to the healthy expression of the Strength polarity

is that personal power is used not only for self-preservation but also to facilitate the well-being of others. Thus the actualizing Christian uses power to edify or build up others, rather than to dominate, intimidate, or exploit them. It is a power made gentle by Christ's love and insulated by the virtue of humility.

One further characteristic of strength is that it enables us to become active participants and creators, with God, in how life turns out for us. When we are in touch with our strength, we do not sit around and gripe, complain, murmur, gossip, or whine. We do something. We take responsibility for shaping our own lives and the world around us. And we pray with Reinhold Niebuhr: Lord, help me to accept the things I cannot change, and change the things that I can. And give me wisdom to know the difference.

EXERCISES

1. How good are you at expressing caring feelings in verbal and physical ways? Have you ever considered that the special people in your life may never know the depth of your love if you do not express it in crystal clear ways? Experiment this week with a little more touching or verbal statements of appreciation or admiration and see what happens.

2. Just as with caring feelings, risk in the near future letting people know how you feel when you are uptight. If it has nothing to do with them, tell them so. If it is related to their behavior, tell them so. Work at developing a diplomatic but still firm style of assertiveness when you sense an injustice going on. Practice the "cash and carry" approach of not letting anger build up inside, but rather letting it out while still a

minor feeling of irritation—open for discussion and the input of other's feelings too.

3. When it comes to vulnerability, ask yourself if you are on any high horse. If so, ask a few other people how and when your pomposity comes out—chances are they will tell you. Quit trying to be "king of the mountain" forever. You have faults—admit them. You make mistakes—confess them. You are human—acknowledge it.

4. It is just as important to get your feelings of strength and confidence going as it is to be sometimes humble and open to correction. Try the "strength bombardment" technique where you ask a few trusted others to bombard you with positive input regarding your life and personality. Soak it up. Take it in—and savor every moment of what was said when you are all alone again.

5. Deliberately practice awareness of the four polarities of personality as well as the reality of the core self all during the weeks and months ahead. Rehearse the concepts. Utilize them all during the day. Master the theory, and make it work for you, enabling you, with God's help, to perfect your life in every way.

14

GROWING TOWARD WHOLENESS

There are many in the Church as well as out of it who need to learn that Christianity is neither a creed nor a ceremonial, but a life vitally connected to a loving Christ.

—*Josiah Strong*

How is it possible that the fears that lie behind the partial perspectives and personality disorders described earlier be healed by the perfect love of God?

We believe that the secret lies in our decision to acknowledge, but never to be defeated by, our weaknesses or failures. The courage of imperfection enables us to live every day, every week with a need for and openness to God's healing love. Our open admission of our weaknesses becomes a royal road to the power of the Holy Spirit within our core. Paul records that after praying three times for a particular weakness to be taken away from him, the Lord replied: "My grace is sufficient for you, for My strength comes to perfection where there is weakness" (2 Corinthians 12:9 MLB).

Rather than denying or fragmenting our humanity, we must embrace it. Neither shame nor arrogance should distract us from the steady growth process that the Holy Spirit carries out in us. Our continued perfection is of our faith. Our faith in God's redeeming grace. Our faith in

Christ's abiding presence. Our faith in the Holy Spirit who guides us from within.

Our faith is not just in God as an awesomely *transcendent* Being, but also as an *immanent* Presence who permeates our whole body, mind, and soul. Because we trust in him—the Ground of all Being—we can also trust our own being, our own core. God has not come into our lives to rob us of an identity or to make of us impersonal pawns for his manipulative use. That is not how love, least of all divine love, works. Rather, he has come to us to affirm, enhance, and fulfill our identities, to make us each unique and different, yet keep us all related and connected to himself and all human beings everywhere. This is the master plan, but our lives center mainly on working out the plan for our particular little corner in the world.

Growing in faith, we learn to trust our core and the power of our combined polarities. We learn to listen to our intuitions, feelings, insights, dreams, promptings, and heart's desires. We learn to trust our God-given intelligence and thinking and reasoning capabilities. We learn to expand our imaginations and creativity. We learn to exercise our wills. We learn to care for our bodies. And we learn to improve and work on our relationships. The divine-human dialogue leads us to these visible results of our invisible power.

The human personality is a garden to be tilled, planted, nurtured, and harvested throughout the seasons of life. As Jesus said, "I have chosen you, and ordained you, that ye should go and bring forth fruit, and that your fruit should remain" (John 15:16 KJV).

The rhythmic flow of the four polarities we have covered, along with a growing trust in the core where our being merges with his being, leads to the fruit of the Spirit-filled personality. But we must remind you that it may take many years or even a lifetime to evolve, with

God's help, this integration. Trusting the growth process, and accepting as a reality each day God's amazing grace, are more important than our attempts to measure our successes or failures all the time. We need not live under the "curse of perfectionism." None of us is or will be in this lifetime perfect. Openness to admit our need for continued growth is all that is required. And, by being very patient and tolerant of ourselves, we will become equally patient and tolerant of others.

We join Paul in saying, "And the very God of peace sanctify you *wholly*; and I pray God your *whole* spirit and soul and body be preserved blameless unto the coming of our Lord Jesus Christ. Faithful is he that calleth you, who also will do it" (1 Thessalonians 5:23-24 KJV, italics ours). This, special reader, is our deepest prayer for you.

An important aspect of our growth as authors is feedback we receive from you, the reader. We are interested in knowing what happens when you apply principles in the book to your life. You may give us personal feedback by writing to us in care of Abingdon Press, 201 Eighth Avenue, South, P.O. Box 801, Nashville, Tennessee 37202. You may direct your letter either to Everett Shostrom or Dan Montgomery, or jointly to both.

BIBLIOGRAPHY

Alberti, Robert, and Michael Emmons. *Your Perfect Right*. San Luis Obisbo, Cal.: Impact Publishers, 1982.

Assagioli, Roberto. *Psychosynthesis*. New York: Viking, 1965.

Berdyaev, Nicholas. *The Realm of Spirit and the Realm of Caesar*. Translated by Donald A. Lowrie. New York: Harper and Brothers, 1952.

Bonhoeffer, Dietrich. *Ethics*. Translated by Eberhard Bethge. New York: Macmillan, 1965.

Brammer, Lawrence, and Everett Shostrom. *Therapeutic Psychology*. Englewood Cliffs, N.J.: Prentice-Hall, 1982.

Clinebell, Charlotte. *Meet Me in the Middle*. New York: Harper and Row, 1973.

Diagnostic and Statistical Manual of Mental Disorders. 3rd ed. Washington, D.C.: American Psychiatric Association, 1980.

Erwin, Gayle. *The Jesus Style*. Waco, Tex.: Word Books, 1983.

Frankl, Viktor. *Man's Search for Meaning*. New York: Simon and Schuster, 1959.

Freud, Sigmund. *A General Introduction to Psychoanalysis*. Translated by Joan Riviere. New York: Simon and Schuster, 1965.

Graham, Billy. *How to Be Born Again*. Waco, Tex.: Word Books, 1977.

Horney, Karen. *Our Inner Conflicts*. New York: W. W. Norton, 1945.

Jung, Carl. *C. G. Jung Speaking*. Edited by McGuire and Hull. Princeton, N.J.: Princeton University Press, 1977.

————. *Memories, Dreams, Reflections*. Edited by Aniela Jaffe. Translated by Richard Winston and Clara Winston. New York: Pantheon Books, 1963.

————. *Psychological Types*. Vol. 6 of *Collected Works of Carl Jung*. Princeton, N.J.: Princeton University Press, 1977.

————. *Psychology and Alchemy*. Vol. 12 of *Collected Works of Carl Jung*. Princeton, N.J.: Princeton University Press, 1974.

Kierkegaard, Søren. *The Journals of Kierkegaard.* Edited by Alexander Dru. New York: Harper and Row, 1959.

Klein, D. F. *Psychiatric Case Studies.* Baltimore: Williams and Wilkins, 1972.

Ladd, George. *A Theology of the New Testament.* Grand Rapids: Eerdmans, 1974.

Leary, T. *Interpersonal Diagnosis of Personality.* New York: The Ronald Press Co., 1957.

Lindbergh, A. M. *Hour of Gold, Hour of Lead.* New York: Harcourt Brace Jovanovich, 1973.

Lowen, Alexander. *Bioenergetics.* New York: Coward, McCann, and Geoghegan, 1975.

———. *Narcissism.* New York: Macmillan, 1983.

Marcel, Gabriel. *Creative Fidelity.* New York: Farrar, Straus, and Giroux, 1964.

Maslow, Abraham. *Motivation and Personality.* 2nd ed. New York: Harper, 1970.

———. *Toward a Psychology of Being.* 2nd ed. New York: Van Nostrand, 1968.

May, Rollo. *Man's Search for Himself.* New York: Dell Publishing Co., 1973.

———. *The Discovery of Being.* New York: W. W. Norton, 1983.

Menninger, Karl A. *Love Against Hate.* New York: Harcourt, Brace, 1959.

Miller, Keith. *A Taste of New Wine.* Waco, Tex.: Word Books, 1964.

———. *Please Love Me.* Waco, Tex.: Word Books, 1977.

Millon, Theodore. *Modern Psychopathology.* Prospect, Ill.: Waveland Press, 1983.

Montagu, Ashley, *Growing Young.* New York: McGraw-Hill, 1981.

Montgomery, Dan. *Courage to Love.* Glendale, Cal.: Regal Books, 1980.

Moreno, Jacobi. *Psychodrama.* Vol. I. New York: Beacon House, 1972.

O'Connor, Elizabeth. *Search for Silence.* Waco, Tex.: Word Books, 1972.

Osborne, Cecil. *The Art of Learning to Love Yourself.* Grand Rapids: Zondervan, 1976.

Reich, Wilhelm. *Character Analysis.* 3rd ed. New York: Farrar, Straus, and Giroux, 1949.

Rogers, Carl R. *On Becoming a Person*. Boston: Houghton Mifflin, 1961.

Runyon, Theodore, ed. *What the Spirit Is Saying to the Churches*. New York: Hawthorn Books, 1975.

Schaeffer, Francis. *True Spirituality*. Wheaton, Ill.: Tyndale House, 1971.

Shostrom, Everett L. *Actualizing Therapy: Foundations for a Scientific Ethic*. San Diego: EDITS, 1976.

————. *From Manipulator to Master*. New York: Bantam Books, 1983.

————. *Man, the Manipulator*. Nashville: Abingdon, 1967.

Shostrom, Everett L., and Dan Montgomery. *Healing Love: How God Works in the Personality*. Nashville: Abingdon, 1978.

Stevens, John, ed. *Gestalt Is*. Moab, Utah: Real People Press, 1975.

Stuart, Grace. *Narcissus: A Psychological Study of Self-Love*. New York: Macmillan, 1955.

Tillich, Paul. *The New Being*. New York: Scribner's, 1955.

————. *The Shaking of the Foundations*. New York: Scribner's, 1948.

Tournier, Paul. *The Adventure of Living*. New York: Harper and Row, 1965.

————. *A Place for You*. New York: Harper and Row, 1968.

————. *The Strong and the Weak*. Philadelphia: Westminster Press, 1963.

Van Kaam, Adrian. *Dynamics of Spiritual Self-Direction*. Denville, N.J.: Dimension Books, 1976.

————. *In Search of Spiritual Identity*. Denville, N.J.: Dimension Books, 1975.

————. *Looking for Jesus*. Denville, N.J.: Dimension Books, 1978.

————. *Spirituality and the Gentle Life*. Denville, N.J.: Dimension Books, 1974.

Vetter, Bernadette. *My Journey, My Prayer*. New York: Wm. H. Sadlier, 1977.

APPENDIX

ACTUALIZING FILMS

The following films, produced or distributed by Everett L. Shostrom, may be ordered to enhance the meaning of *God in Your Personality* when the book is used to stimulate discussion in group settings such as church retreats, community college or university classrooms, group psychotherapy, or church related groups. To request a complete catalog of these and other films, write Psychological and Education Films, 3334 East Coast Hwy., # 252, Corona Del Mar, CA, 92625.

Between Man and Woman. 16mm. Color. 33 minutes.

In conversation with Howard Miller, Everett L. Shostrom discusses six manipulative relating patterns found in most marriages, and utilizes professional actors to demonstrate these modes of relating.

The Actualization Group. Seven-film series. 16mm. Black and white. 45 minutes each.

This series follows one group through seven sequential sessions of therapy with Everett L. Shostrom and Nancy Ferry. Each session focuses on a different general theme: "Risking Being Ourselves," "Freedom and Actualization," "Aggression and Actualization," "Manipulation and Actualization," "The Divorce from Parents," "Self-Disclosure of the Therapist," and "From Deadness to Aliveness."

Rollo May and Human Encounter: Self-Self Encounter and Self-Other Encounter. 16mm. Color. 30 minutes.

May describes the human dilemma as having to see yourself as both subject and object in life, and discusses the four elements of human encounter: empathy, eros, friendship, and agape.

Rollo May and Human Encounter: Manipulation and Human Encounter—Exploitation of Sex. 16mm. Color. 30 minutes.

May discusses how manipulation occurs when any of the four elements of human encounter is missing, the problem of transference in psychotherapy as a distortion of human encounter, and modern man's fixation on sexuality.

Touching: Importance for Human Growth. 16mm. Color. 29 minutes.

A conversation with Ashley Montagu on the key concepts of his recent work, *Touching.* Utilizing psychological research and medical opinion,

Montagu develops the case that touching is necessary for human life, and especially vital for intimate human communication.

Maslow and Self-Actualization, Film no. 1. 16mm. Color. 30 minutes.

Abraham Maslow discusses honesty and awareness as dimensions of self-actualization and elaborates on recent research and theory related to each.

Maslow and Self-Actualization, Film no. 2. 16mm. Color. 30 minutes.

A continuation of the previous film. Maslow discusses self-actualization in terms of the dimensions of freedom and trust and examines recent research and theory related to them.

Target Five, Film no. 1. 16mm. Color. 26 minutes.

Virginia Satir and Everett L. Shostrom discuss and role-play manipulative responses commonly found in marriage and family relating.

Target Five, Film no. 2. 16mm. Color. 22 minutes.

Satir and Shostrom describe and role-play three essential qualities of an actualizing relationship.

A Conversation with Carl Rogers. 16mm. Black and white. 31 minutes.

In conversation with Keith Berwick, Rogers comments on humanistic psychology, his own Client-Centered Therapy, and the value of encounter groups in today's society.

Frankl and the Search for Meaning. 16mm. Color. 30 minutes.

Viktor Frankl describes man's search for meaning as a form of "height" psychology, as opposed to Freudian theory, which he describes as "depth" psychology. Frankl says that, in his continuous growth toward self-actualization, each person must keep revising old assumptions and discovering new meanings for his or her self.

Three Approaches to Psychotherapy I. 16mm. Color. 48/32/38 minutes each.

A classic film series, also known as the *Gloria Films*, presents the compelling paradoxes and conflicts between what we are, what we believe, and the way we behave. Gloria, in therapy sessions with Carl Rogers, Frederick Perls, and Albert Ellis, seeks answers, discovers new questions, and perhaps finds a greater understanding of herself through Rogers' Client Centered Therapy, Perls Gestalt Therapy, and Ellis' Rational-Emotive Therapy.

Three Approaches to Psychotherapy II. 16mm. Color. 45 minutes each.

This three-part film focuses on a young woman, Kathy, who is trying to learn more actualizing responses for dealing with the men in her life. The film reveals how three distinct approaches to therapeutic psychology are brought to bear on her difficulties. The therapists are Carl Rogers (Client-Centered Therapy), Everett L. Shostrom (Actualizing Therapy), and Arnold Lazarus (Multi-Modal Therapy), respectively.

INDEX